Active atmospheres are (pink donuts) in hybrid modes.

Pamphlet Architecture 37
Active Atmospheres:
On Instruments and Protocols for Medium
Hybrids and Architectural Voids
Catty Dan Zhang | Temporary Office

Steven Myron Holl Foundation
Station Hill Press

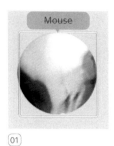

Mouse

01

Test 1.1 Filters Applied

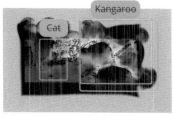

Kangaroo

Cat

02

Test 2.1 Vents

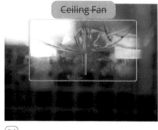

Ceiling Fan

04

Test 1.2 War Theater

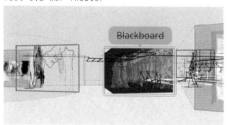

Blackboard

03

04-07	08-09	10-25
Introduction	**Conversation**	**Experiments**
Medium Matters, Or All That Needs to Be Relabled	On Mediums: From Human Perception Onward	Set 1: Particulates along Motion Axes
01	w/ Rebecca Uchill	02 03

Test 2.2 Fans

Moon

Bird

05

Test 2.3 Masks Car

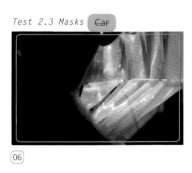

06

Mobile Phone

08 *Test 3.2 Interior Cities*

Test 3.1 Webcams+

Tent

07

Test 3.3 Collaborate-vision Machines

Lawn Mower

09

26–47	*48–73*	*74–78*
Experiments	**Experiments**	**Conversation**
Set 2: Moving Air Systems	Set 3: Video Captures and Screen Shares	On Technological Models: Toward Something Big
04 05 06	07 08 09	w/ Orit Halpern

Medium Matters

Or All That Needs to Be Relabeled

Human beings and machines, as well as all kinds of other nonhuman agents, not only actively connect but also intersect through this ethereal yet material topology. A space of mixture and communicative exchange between the very substance of beings, this airy atmosphere is the ultimate medium....To live in a society is to take part in constructing an atmosphere, in creating "the air" of a place. It also means taking responsibility for this climate: for the air that we breathe in and out, and breathe within.

—Giuliana Bruno, "In the Air: Atmospheric Thinking"

During the very early morning of May 5, 2016, I went for a walk wearing a portable optical apparatus, taking perceptual measurements of human mobility while interacting with visible air movements. This device measures a space of two feet in length, ten inches in width, and a foot and a half in height. It was made so that one

0.1

0.2

Fig 0.1. *Medium Matters*, 2016, a wearable hot-air visualizer for seeing heat with the naked eyes

Fig 0.2. View of *Medium Matters* at the Pamphlet Architecture exhibition, 'T' Space, Rhinebeck, NY, September 2022

Fig 0.3. Still-frame excerpt from the video documentation of hot air visualized during a walking test of the device

Fig 0.4. Diagram of the perceptual mediation in the void space between the eye and the visible forms in the built environment

could carry it around and see hot air with the naked eye. The walk happened along my daily walking route. The path was no more than one thousand feet in distance, yet the walk lasted about eight minutes. This speed of roughly 1.5 miles per hour—less than half of the average walking pace of an adult—had little to do with the minute extra weight on my head. Rather, a drastically altered perception of the built environment—the otherwise invisible forms of heat morphing intensely with both one's own movements and atmospheric dynamics—impacted the body sensorium as an ensemble.

The hot-air visualizer assembles a pair of parabolic mirrors at a specific distance from each eye and, with techniques of "bending light," detects the subtle changes in the air density caused by convection activities due to the temperature differences in the atmosphere. As a result, it captures thin volumes of air movements that are visually cropped into two circles two feet in front of the retina. A scientific tool in nature, it is a perception device that overlays the movements of the hot air in the foreground with the surrounding environment that changes in perspective as the background, both which take place because of one's own movement. The wearable instrument is thus a temporal device that signifies the sense of motion and makes one aware of the perception of time. Human vision becomes a medium that, through a visual parallax of two scales and intensities of movements, records the perceptual dynamism of the void spaces between the eye and the visible forms in the built environment.

Titled *Medium Matters*, the instrument invites a discovery of the unseen. Zooming out from the two circular visible areas of hot air, the "unseen" here is not merely a visibility property. Rather, it suggests

already been supporters of the invisible for a long time"; art critic and painter John Ruskin concluded from fifty years of accurately recorded observations that the darkening of the sky in Europe in the nineteenth century was a result of industrial pollution; architect and scholar Adrian Lahoud called attention to the loosening bond between the contact and the trace in forensic studies caused by the earth's climate and that "it breaks the link between attribution, responsibility, and, potentially, justice"; artist Trevor Paglen explored the new "invisible visuality" in a visual culture detached from human eyes due to rapid technological development and uncovered how intelligent machine systems ingest images into a massive AI training set for accurate recognition that

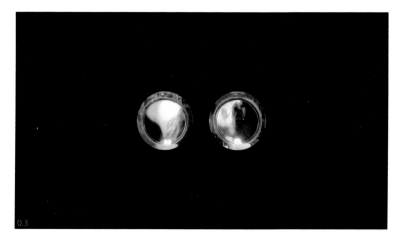

0.3

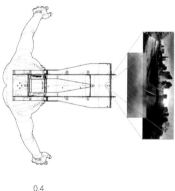

0.4

a temporary status before things are perceived and events are noticed—the rising of temperature before glaciers start disappearing, the spreading of viruses before symptoms present in crowds, the silent machine-to-machine communications before visual signals become images overloading the media network, to name a few examples. It's been the interest of many designers and researchers throughout history that the recording and revealing of the process of things becoming seen have served as critical ways to approach the design and analysis of architecture. Italian poet Gabriele D'Annunzio recognized the richest experience happening before we take notice, that "when we begin to open our eyes to the visible, we have

ultimately influence the everyday life via the internet.[1] In capturing and appropriating the unseen, we recognize the built environment as fields filled with hidden networks and imperceptible mediums and as active atmospheres that constantly adapt, react, and mutate. With or without humans as a part, architecture today is situated simultaneously within these fields and beyond the geography-specific context.

Yet pressing issues that we face nowadays in terms of environmental, social, and technological realities urge instantaneousness in registering the unseen status to approach architectural productions in a timely and responsible manner—at the speed of real time. Shaped by active conditions, architecture has undergone different theoretical and technological considerations that have shifted from the fixed to the dynamic, from the stable to the impermanent, and from "becoming temporal" to "being spontaneous." These are fundamentally relational transformations through which individuals connect to and exchange with the world in ways that are mobilized and animated. Architecture can thus be explored through typological opportunities that foreground the design of active systems, assembling temporalities and relations rather than mediating formal and material logics. In architectural historian Antoine Picon's observations on animation and materiality in his recent book *The Materiality of Architecture*, technical devices and

us to have the understanding and relating actions and their impacts—the agency that we need to have as citizens living in society today—with immediacy. From a direct interaction between a walker and the hot air to an invisible tie between virus outbreaks and their social consequences, and so on—we seek ways to articulate and innovate upon the bond between actions and the physical world across scales, locations, and time. Rather than simply turning to the emergence of tools that trend toward possibly more effective, more efficient, and more intelligent capacities of responding to urgent challenges we have been facing, we must instead recognize that our radically mutated intimacy with technology, objects, and mediums demands

Fig 0.5. Methodological framework of active atmospheres: integrating medium hybrids and visual techniques for various design experiments, from responsive environments to multimedia and extended reality

Fig 0.6. Typological explorations of the three sets of design experiments

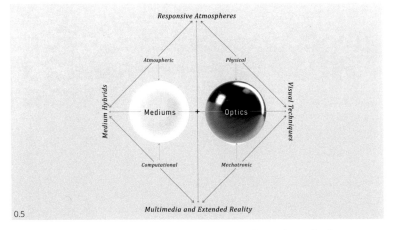

0.5

objects that affect humans and the physical world—from steam engine to the Internet of Things—have led to wide-ranging assessments and broader concepts of materiality than ones that strictly relate to building materials and structural techniques.[2] In this regard, architecture is inseparable from the concept of it as a technological framework. And the process of design, while continuously supported by material and system strategies for the physical world, is also becoming a translation of the networked technological interfaces into synergistic spatial instruments that visualize and modulate intangible forms and ephemeral imageries.

Such conceptual corelevance of technical operations and architectural considerations allows

ongoing critical renegotiation and retooling in processes of design. This might require a foundational practice of scrutinizing techniques and mediums that are integral parts of today's digital culture. Web portals, data outlets, cultural objects, raster data, vector attributes, and color fields are a few examples that could serve as both conceptual and technical frameworks. Architectural manifestations would then be derived from the rigorous transformation and hybridization of such cultural and technological familiarities, in which pixels become surfaces, datasets become columns, and interfaces become thresholds—making the digital interchangeable with the material and blurring the distinction between physical environments and technological instruments.

Design thus becomes the process of translating the known means into new mediums, empowering the familiar and normative to become impactful elements and spaces that reveal different forms of human interactions or the intelligence of the nonhuman.

This pamphlet explores applied visual techniques that challenge conventional definitions of tools, measurements, and material forms. Building upon the hybridization of physical and computational mediums and in relation to physical or mechatronic optical systems, it views architectural production as more void and intangible than solid and concrete; more synthesized and networked than spatial and formal; more of layers Multiply than of Boolean subtraction;

design vision, probing the paradigm shift into possible futures.

Perpetually active, atmospheres support the production of conditions that emerge as ephemeral voids, ambiguous partitions, and fuzzy edges—a few topologies explored in this pamphlet—through the endless process of recording and revealing. No final forms, constantly approximating. Vulnerable systems and all forms of activities—lurking in the unseen— become the raw materials of architecture. In an era of overflowing emergencies, we need to continuously build awareness of these different forms of materials and perpetually reinterpret the dominant modes of technological operations. In the end, designing

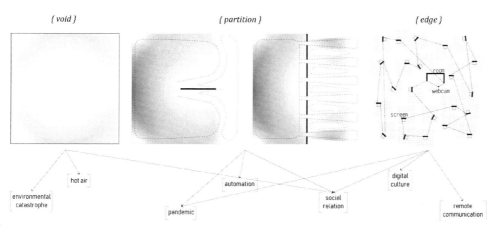

{ void } { partition } { edge }

0.6

more medium hybrids modulated than air-conditioned. Categorized into three sets, a total of eight design experiments respond to the present urgencies around the air we breathe, the data we exchange, the image we consume—through industrial, mechanical, domestic, and virtual platforms. Each experiment in this issue is grounded scientifically—simulated, prototyped, and/or built. They resist the symbolic representation of machine and system; they celebrate the interplay between accurate behavior and indeterminate effects. Part technical operations, part theorizing technology through architectural logics, these works appropriate new frameworks to make relevance of what we do today with technological potentialities and the grounded

architecture is itself a medium for constructing active atmospheres.

[notes]

1   John Ruskin, *The Storm-Cloud of the Nineteenth Century: Two Lectures Delivered at the London Institution February 4th and 11th, 1884* (Sunnyside, Orpington, Kent: George Allen, 1884); Andrian Lahoud, "Floating Bodies," in *Forensis: The Architecture of Public Truth,* ed. Eyal Weizman and Anselm Franke (Berlin: Sternberg, 2014), 495–518; Trevor Paglen, "Invisible Images: Your Pictures Are Looking at You," *Architectural Design* 89.1 (2019), 22–27.

2   Antoine Picon, *The Materiality of Architecture* (Minneapolis: University of Minnesota Press, 2020), 71.

On Mediums: From Human Perception Onward

In Conversation with Rebecca Uchill

[conceptualizing mediums]

Catty Dan Zhang: In the book *Experience: Culture, Cognition, and Common Sense*, you discussed "technology mediating experience—whether by machines or mediums of our very bodily sensorium."[1] The mediation of modern life and human-perception-as-medium seems to be a good place to start our conversation and trace the historical and present links between technology, experience, and human subjectivity. Both in that particular context and overall, how would you define/conceptualize mediums?

Rebecca Uchill: The question of "what is a medium" is one that I examined in the "Mediating" essay prefacing *Experience: Culture, Cognition, and the Common Sense*. The essay looks at *G: Material zur Elementaren Gestaltung* [G: Material for elemental form-creation], a Weimar Republic artists journal published by avant-garde filmmaker Hans Richter out of Berlin in the early 1920s. I was interested in the contributors' theorizations of technology as a sort of corrective to the shortfalls of subjectivity. The idea, and nomenclature, of medium is complex in that context—in the essay, I refer to Germanist Tobias Wilke's work discussing the more common use of the term *Mittel*, or "means." Wilke is particularly concerned with cultural theorist Walter Benjamin's use of the term, and his introduction of the word *medium* in relation to human perception.[2]

I believe that I wanted to use the essay to define the concept of a medium relationally—always, in some sense, mediated and a mediating device unto itself. That felt important in composing an introductory essay to a volume like *Experience*, in which I did not want to suggest the existence of anything like a universal experience (despite, or perhaps more rightly in light of, the subtitle's inclusion of the phrase "common sense"). Experiences are not only sensorially and socially constructed but also structurally. That premise underlies my overarching research focus on institutional histories of art and culture, particularly the

histories of museums and other entities that are stewards of cultural production, preservation, and interpretation. It is within such structured spaces of experience that canons are constructed and that decisions are made about which literal materials, for example, might be prioritized in conservation and archival activities: in other words, legacies of experience are also produced here. These spaces are, categorically, mediators, and understanding how they function helps us to understand how cultures are conveyed (defined) between past and present, or between curator and audience.

[mediating mediums]

CDZ: I remember when *Experience* came out, it was really exciting that, both as a volume of knowledge and as an artifact, it established an active dialogue with readers through the manifestation of mediated experiences. And with different kinds of activities related to reading, in many ways, it bridged the "visual or representational" and the "critical sensory apparatus" with embedded technologies in a broader sense. Could you talk about the book as a curatorial piece—to be held in one's hand—in relation to mediation and mediums?

RU: I was brought into the editorial team in my role as a Mellon postdoctoral fellow at MIT's interdisciplinary Center for Art, Science & Technology. It was important to me that artists invited to participate in this volume should be given the same opportunity to publish fully-realized work as, say, a neuroscientist or anthropologist. As curator of artist entries, I started to think about artists whose work at the time was interrogating the notion of experience in some form and who could produce work that could be manifest materially in a printed book. This was definitely an exercise in thinking about the mediating capacities of the book as medium!

The contributions were quite diverse, and ambitious. The composer Alvin Lucier created a score for the volume that turned the book into an instrument. We had a whole team working to support artist Carsten Höller's proposal to integrate synthesized human pheromones into inks printed in the designs on the endpapers.[3] Renée Green, an artist, writer, and filmmaker, shared designs, notes, and notebook entries with the intention that readers move off the printed page and into the world—both physical and online—to research the phrases and ideas cited in her offering.

[materializing mediums]

CDZ: While *Experience* resonates with the significance of *G: Material zur Elementaren Gestaltung* that embraced mediation, *Being Material*—the symposium and publication that you coorganized and coedited—categorizes how we relate bits and atoms in different ways today and argues that "the activity of being digital is entrenched in its conditions of being material."[4] As human agency is reshaped by technology and materiality and as we live in the "hybrid of being digital-material," I was wondering if you could reflect upon human-perception-as-medium from the perspective of the material world—with human inputs as a part, as well as the lives and impacts of materials beyond human factors.

RU: The *Being Material* volume that followed in 2019 segued quite directly into the digital realm, with the use of a cover design and insert that interact with camera phones to link to companion material hosted at beingmaterial.mit.edu. This design, moving between atoms and bits, was coordinated by an amazing team of E Roon Kang and Minkyoung Kim of Math Practice, with Skylar Tibbits, Marcelo Coelho, and Lukas Debiasi of MIT's Self-Assembly Lab. My rather limited involvement with the website was in the form of coauthoring an addendum to the "Livable" section of the volume with anthropologist and writer Stefan Helmreich, in which we did indeed reflect on posthuman epistemes and other areas of "new materialism." Our addendum addressed structural matters of exclusion, marginalization, exploitation, and complicity at MIT that were revealed shortly after the book's publication.[5] At issue here is that human-individual scales of experience are very much materially inscribed within the superstructure.

    G was reductive in its forecasting, I would say. Today, it is quite evident that there is, in fact, a complex and relational dynamic in which the human agent mediates the digital form, and vice versa, with very material effects. Hito Steyerl, a filmmaker and moving-image artist, recently published a piece in *New Left Review* showing how market logics directly and concretely skew machine learning and human experience. She points to a "white box algorithm, or social filter" that is reproduced in machine outputs. I may be naive in hoping that everyday people retain some level of control over the generation and application of such "human factors," to point back to your question. Steyerl suggests that this means "untrain[ing] oneself from a system of multiple extortion and extraction."[6] This sounds near impossible, but I am holding optimistically to the notion that we have the ability to radically reshape our systems and our institutions—which are imperfect, but they are the ones we have created. Art and other mediums of cultural productions not only reflect our world back to us but retain strong powers of persuasion and, with these capacities, the ability to materially rethink and retool our worlds.

[notes]

1   Rebecca Uchill, "Mediating," in *Experience: Culture, Cognition, and the Common Sense*, ed. Caroline Jones, David Mather, and Rebecca Uchill (Cambridge, MA: MIT Press, 2016), 35–66.

2   Tobias Wilke, "Tacti(ca)lity Reclaimed: Benjamin's Medium, the Avant-Garde, and the Politics of the Senses," *Grey Room* 39 (Spring 2010): 39.

3   Stefanie Hessler, Rebecca Uchill, and Carsten Höller, "Pattern Recognition: A Background for Carsten Höller's Smelling Dots (Portrait of Cedric Price), 2016," *Future Anterior: Journal of Historic Preservation, History, Theory, and Criticism* 13, no. 2 (Winter 2016), 45–55, https://doi.org/10.5749/futuante.13.2.0045.

4   Marie-Pier Boucher, Stefan Helmreich, Leila W Kinney, Skylar Tibbits, Rebecca Uchill, and Evan Ziporyn eds., *Being Material* (Cambridge, MA: MIT Press, 2019).

5   Rebecca Uchill and Stefan Helmreich, "Addendum," in *Being Material*, ed. Marie-Pier Boucher, Stefan Helmreich, Leila W. Kinney, Skylar Tibbits, Rebecca Uchill, and Evan Ziporyn (Cambridge, MA: MIT Press, 2019), https://beingmaterial.mit.edu/livable/addendum.

6   Hito Steyerl, "Mean Images" *New Left Review* 140/141 (May/June 2023), https://newleftreview.org/issues/ii140/articles/hito-steyerl-mean-images.

Rebecca Uchill is the director of Center for Art, Design, and Visual Culture at the College of Arts, Humanities and Social Sciences, University of Maryland, Baltimore County.

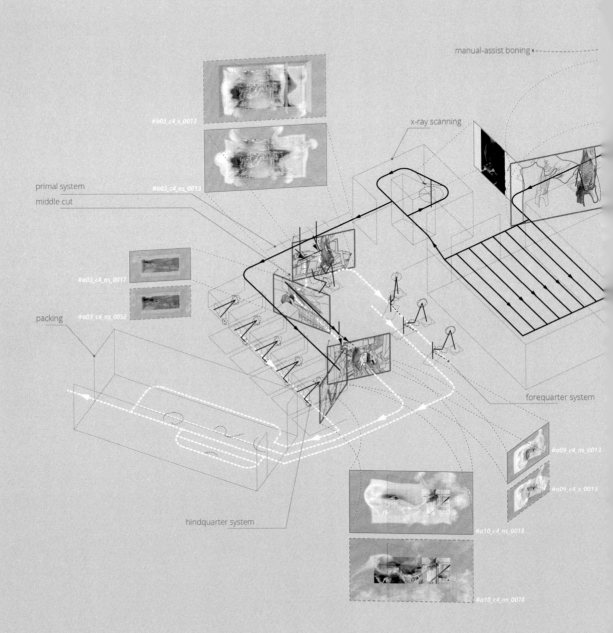

manual-assist boning ◄- - - - - - - - - - -

x-ray scanning

#b03_c4_s_0013

#b03_c4_ns_0013

primal system
middle cut

#a03_c4_ns_0017

packing

#a03_c4_ns_0052

forequarter system

#a09_c4_ns_0013

#a09_c4_s_0013

hindquarter system

#a10_c4_ns_0018

#a10_c4_ns_0078

SET 1: Particulates along Motion Axes

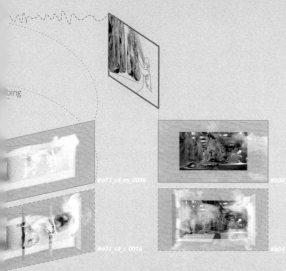

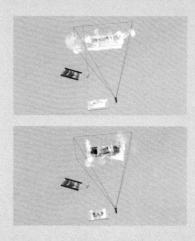

In Peter Sloterdijk's book *Terror from the Air*, he argues that the contemporary fragmentation of the atmosphere and individualized breathing space threatens social synthesis and humanity and turns the atmosphere into a "war theater."[1] Sloterdijk's criticism reveals the consequences of architectural technologies that focus on conditioned space and sealed weather; nevertheless, providing inhabitants a protected relationship with the matter of air has been the fundamental drive in almost all aspects of architectural productions. While in some cases clear boundaries are implemented for a controlled environment, in other situations they are ephemeral—revealing, reacting to, or even activating their external environmental and social conditions. The perception of such boundary situations has radically altered amid the pandemic, during which the concerns of health and safety within the void spaces correlate with invisible subdivisions using a six-foot diameter of spatial measurement, such as with temporary shields, or by the reduction or elimination of human presence.

Meat-processing plants became hot spots during the COVID-19 pandemic due to the transmission of invisible particles within the public void and across species. In industries that have historically relied on human labor, the coronavirus outbreak resulted in temporary operational pivots much more chaotic and drastic than ones witnessed before. *Set 1* employs multimedia approaches to rethink industrial big boxes as combinatory relationships of particulates and motion axes and to make a case for automation and humanity.

Test 1.1:
Filters Applied
[computational tools]

Test 1.2:
War Theater
[staged narratives]

1   Peter Sloterdijk,
Terror from the Air (Los Angeles:
Semiotext(e), 2009).

[setups/linkages]

Paths through Forms

We began to understand that man is not only what he eats, but what he breathes and that in which he is immersed. Cultures are collective conditions of immersion in air and sign systems.

—Peter Sloterdijk, *Terror from the Air*

[tracing]

The mechanization of modern assembly lines in the early twentieth century employed measures of quantifying time and motion in the human work process for efficiency and productivity. Famously revealed by Frank B. Gilbreth, an American engineer and pioneer of scientific management, with chronocyclegraphs, optical traces appearing in black-and-white photographs with various curve configurations were documentations of absolute paths of movements as workers repetitively

1.1

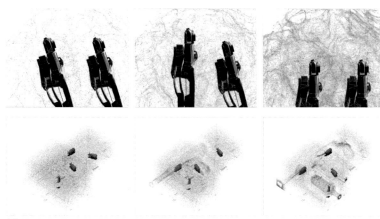

1.2

Fig 1.1. Frank and Lillian Gilbreth, *Motion Efficiency Study*, c. 1914. Frank and Lillian Gilbreth Collection, Archives Center, National Museum of American History, Smithsonian Institution.

Figs 1.2-1.3. *Test 1.1 Filters Applied*, simulated paths of moving subjects (animals, robots, humans) through particle blobs

performed specific tasks. The visual quantifications of motion efficiency have since become critical instruments that scientifically informed the spatial layouts of production infrastructures.[1]

In many ways, every invisible boundary in space can be identified by the range of the "reach." Whereas the reach of human hands in repetitive motion sequences as such defines the limits of an individual's areas and the distances between workers and machines, the reach of small droplets or aerosols carrying viruses in the air—in a much different context and scale—sets basis for establishing health and safety restrictions related to exposure duration and proximity to infected persons for controlling the spread of diseases.

Architectures of logistics identify the point where these two types of invisible boundaries intersect and react to each other. Just as architect Eyal Weizman, in *Forensic Architecture*, describes bomb clouds as "airborne cemeteries of architecture and flesh" where survivors breathe in "pulverized life," air along assembly lines is a mixed medium with gasified byproducts that are created as a result of their contact with the sorting, cutting, sawing, and drilling machines.[2] While consumers are provided with various types of end products, workers along the line breathe a form of them in. Mechanical forces from both human and machine operations brutally distribute the contaminated air beyond the safe proximity set for generic conditions, becoming invisible weapons that invade the open spaces within the enclosed facilities.

Set 1 consists of critical representational explorations that unveil spatial effects produced by invisible mediums in motion. Like scientific visualizations of motion of the early twentieth

nonhuman inhabitants, resulting in patterns of actuated currents of particles along fused paths of robot-arm trajectories, livestock movements, kinetic objects, and heat convections. *Test 1.2 War Theater* stages simulated visuals of atmospherically subdivided forms and spaces, labor effects, and temporary safety practices in categorized production segments. Through examining how airflow, meat, and machines act upon each other within industrial big boxes, the project brings the weaponized invisible mediums that laborers inhabit to the forefront through immersive spatial sequences and narratives.

1.3

century, this set of experiments traces paths that intersect with geometries yet also seeks creative and articulated ways of adding medium and atmosphere to the equation. Through documenting, abstracting, reinterpreting, and reconstructing meat-processing and packaging lines based on parameters of multiuse, labor arrangement, and safety regulation, *Set 1* produces visual instruments and virtual scenarios that trace ephemeral spatial volumes and barriers through the visibility of the digital air.

Test 1.1 Filters Applied constructs computational tools that blur the line between the forensic and the imaginary. These exploratory setups identify key relationships between volumes of air and human or

[thresholding]

In 1969, during the transition from Taylorism's advocacy for a system of scientific management in factories to a post-Fordism's notion of "immaterial labor" and flexible production, architect and theoretician Hans Hollein built his Mobile Office, which explored the social and architectural possibilities brought on by the advancement of new technologies. A TV performance two minutes and twenty seconds long staged a new type of laborer within this environmentally enclosed but visually permeable boundary.[3] In 2020, meat-processing facilities installed temporary shields to comply with the OSHA's *Guidance on Preparing Workplaces for COVID-19* and to protect laborers from the shared air. Known as "social distancing dividers," these temporary architectural setups in general public spaces (offices, hotel lobbies, etc.)—typically in clear materials—signaled an environmental and social synthesis similar to the one in Hollein's transparent sphere, simultaneously isolating the single user from the immediate surrounding air pathways but allowing for visible relations toward the other side in the new physical reality. Yet in logistical facilities, arrays of such dividers participate as parts of porous and ephemeral boundaries formed by systems, machineries, and workers that operate their repetitive actions at constant speed over time and in contact with moving particles. These porous edges result in filtered flow forms, aggregating within connected void spaces and becoming dynamic partitions that interrupt the initially homogenous volumes of air. Architecturally, such edges thus serve as filters that regulate the environmental conditions and, by extension, the social, cultural, and political effects that are imposed on inhabitants within the industrial big boxes.

Today, *filter* often refers to the predominant interest in media culture with appearance-altering capacities. On the mechanical side, it entails a partial removal of substances and a reduction of the contents of a compound. Possessing both technical and cultural functions, the filter in this set of works is explored as a form and image operation in unveiling the morphological pattern of invisible forces and particle movements. *Test 1.1* experiments with the coupling of airflow and objects in motion to construct hybrid filters as an augmentation process to reveal and typologize layered visual information. In some cases, operations take literal approaches: layers of porous surfaces, morphing and transforming in scripted sequences, result in modulated segmentation of digital smoke patterns. Some other setups practice a much more comprehensive method that engages the principle of the filter algorithmically, combining object/air and image/air interplays to translate complex scenarios into articulated geometry and force relationships.

Working with computational physics and materiality, these visual instruments explore the gaming of virtual geometries, material attributes, and raster datasets. Particulates drift within the open space, encountering other forces along their journey, settling, and leaving long traces before dissipating. Here, digital air is

considered as spatial, sensorial, and psychological measures, transcribing violent particulate events generated by highly scripted production operations.

[staging]

In political scientist Timothy Pachirat's book *Every Twelve Second*, he observes that "the slaughterhouse is not a single place at all [and that] its internal divisions create physical, linguistic, and phenomenological walls that often feel every bit as rigid as those marking off the exterior of the slaughterhouse from the outside world."[4] Visualizing the air partitioning within air-conditioned spaces signifies such invisible walls as artifacts of industrial culture. While *Test 1.1* builds toward a method for probing the transformations of the meat-processing industry instigated by the public health crisis, *Test 1.2* further expands the exploration by assembling segmented visual outcomes into two thematic scenarios: *Act 1* showcases particle simulations of typical areas within small-scale slaughterhouses viewed in a web-based immersive environment, and *Act 2* composites the architectural phenomena of informal temporary dividers and machine operations. Slicing spaces into planes of air, *Act 2* provides visual agency for rethinking logistic layouts that consist of rigid partitions and labor arrangements and allows motion sets for performing various tasks to become active spatial modulators.

With a digital approach, *Test 1.2* pays homage to Hollein's Mobile Office TV performance through the staging of laborers. Since the COVID-19 pandemic, we've witnessed another significant transition period for the labor organization in the industry. Architectural historian Mario Carpo argues in his recent essay "Design and Automation at the End of Modernity: The Teachings of the Pandemic" that the next wave of robotic fabrication will not automate the industrial factory; instead, it will replace it with a network of smarter, nimbler, reprogrammable facilities with locally sourced materials and energy and will reinvent the preindustrial artisan instead of replacing the industrial worker.[5] In the transition toward the networked and the distributed of the present moment, we need to consider how can we rethink "mental, physical, and sensory well-being" by repurposing labor (high-tech labors),

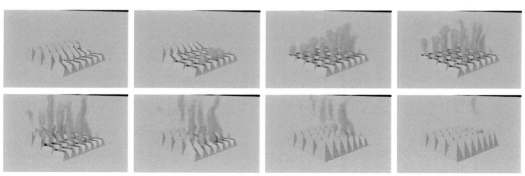

sequence 1

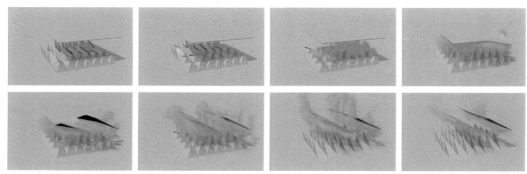

sequence 2

sequence 3

Fig 1.4. *Test 1.1 Filters Applied*, initial animation sketches of constructing ephemeral volumes and boundaries with air movements and collision objects in motion

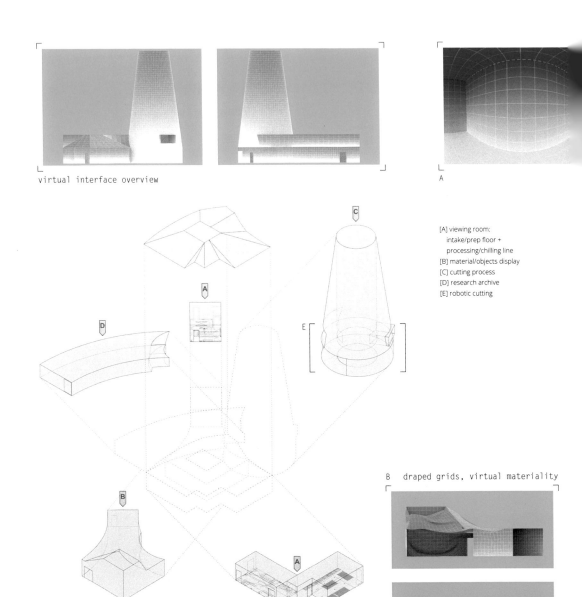

virtual interface overview

A

[A] viewing room:
   intake/prep floor +
   processing/chilling line
[B] material/objects display
[C] cutting process
[D] research archive
[E] robotic cutting

B   draped grids, virtual materiality

Fig 1.5. *Test 1.2 War
Theater, Act 1*, staging
laborer and labor effects

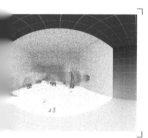

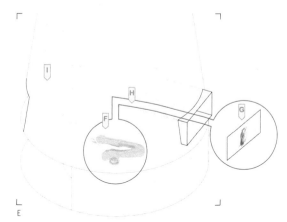

[F] mechanical proces
[G] motion-path extraction
[H] viewing axis
[I] observation area

C

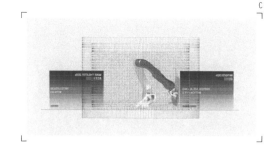

E

decentralizing packaging facilities (microfactories), and inviting public engagement (inhabitable infrastructure)? And how might these radically transformed relations lead to different ways of considering architecture as performative and synergistic systems that modulate the atmosphere we share?[6]

While asking these questions, the act of staging in *Test 1.2* centers around small pieces and subtle details of the nonhuman. Labor effects are depicted through thin slices of the digital air, traces of motion, fluctuations of particulates, and the virtual instability of materials that manifest the invisible intensity of the movements of the air. Wandering within these virtual interfaces, one will encounter draped grids, material failures, scattered baskets, particle storms, and so on—a visual kit of the ephemerals that participate in the vulnerable meat-processing infrastructure. Digitally performing on the screen, these fragments of the kit collectively provoke reflection on what the architecture of production facilities needs to become.

[notes]

1   Sigfried Giedion, *Mechanization Takes Command* (Minneapolis: University of Minnesota Press, 2013), 101–6.

2   Eyal Weizman, *Forensic Architecture: Violence at the Threshold of Detectability* (New York: Zone Books, 2018), 193.

3   Mackenzie Goldberg, "Screen/Print #66: Hans Hollein's Mobile Office and the New Workers' Reality," Archinect, April 2018, https://archinect.com/features/article/150057955/screen-print-66-hans-hollein-s-mobile-office-and-the-new-workers-reality.

4   Timothy Pachirat, *Every Twelve Seconds* (New Haven, CT: Yale University Press, 2013), 236.

5   Mario Carpo, "Design and Automation at the End of Modernity: The Teachings of the Pandemic," *ARIN* 1, no. 3 (2022), https://doi.org/10.1007/s44223-022-00001-0.

6   For more on "mental, physical, and sensory well-being," see "A Lung for Midtown Manhattan: Cedric Price's Entry to the IFCCA Prize Competition for the Design of Cities, 1999," Canadian Center for Architecture, accessed July 27, 2023, https://www.cca.qc.ca/en/articles/77269/a-lung-for-midtown-manhattan.

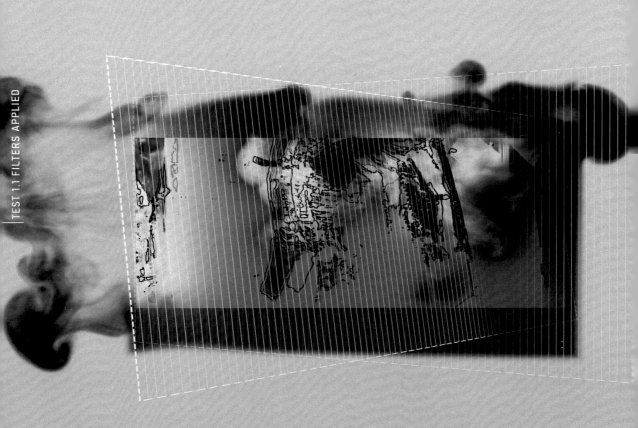

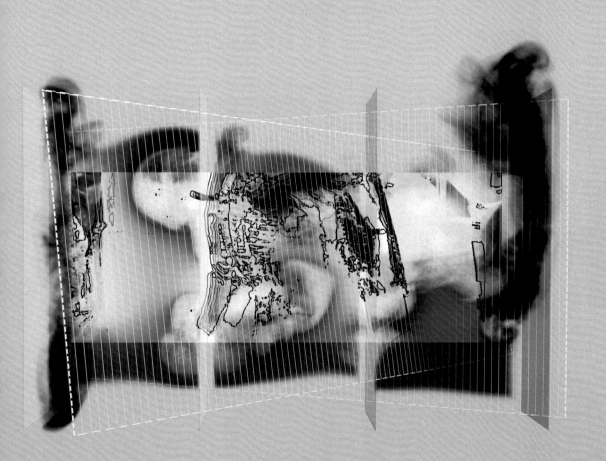

Fig 1.6. *Test 1.1 Filters Applied,* 2021

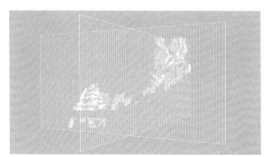 

motion extraction

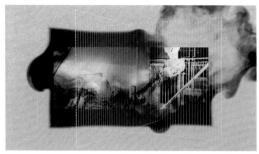 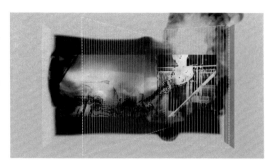

motion/air interaction

 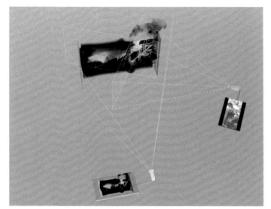

instrument setup

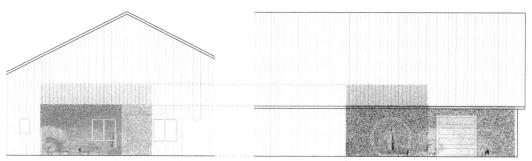

pens/kill floor, side view   pens/kill floor, front view

[note 1.1]

Motion paths extracted from
architectural drawings or video
documentations are translated into
force parameters. Actuated currents
of particles fluctuate along fused paths
within typical killing and processing
compartments, becoming spatial
partitions that constantly vary in
intensity and velocity.

Fig 1.7. [opposite] Image/object
hybrid filters as air-drawing
instruments

Fig 1.8. Orthographic drawings
of tracing atmospheric
subdivisions along processing
lines of a standard red-meat
plant

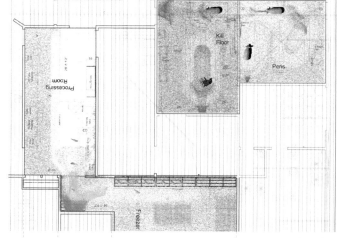

plan view

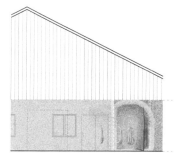

processing/freezer, side view

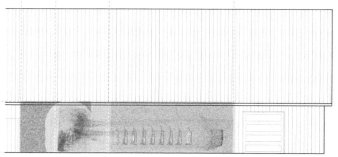

processing/freezer, front view

TEST 1.2 WAR THEATER

force axis

Fig 1.9. *Test 1.2 War Theater, Act 1,* 2023

middle cut

middle cut

[note 1.2]

An automated processing facility is depicted as a set of motion axes of machines performing various scripted tasks over the flow of products being treated. Saws, robots, conveyor belts, rails, and so on—shown as central axes and radii of their movable segments—intersect with sliced views and sliced air volumes. This depiction is a representational apparatus that assembles physics and geometry as spatial systems that foregrounds laborer and labor effects.

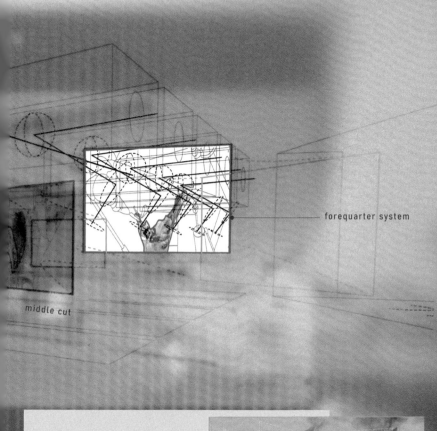

forequarter system

middle cut

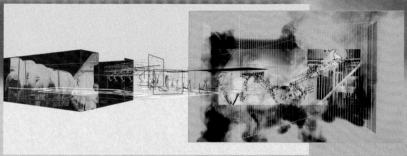

Fig 1.10. *Test 1.2 War Theater, Act 2, 2023*

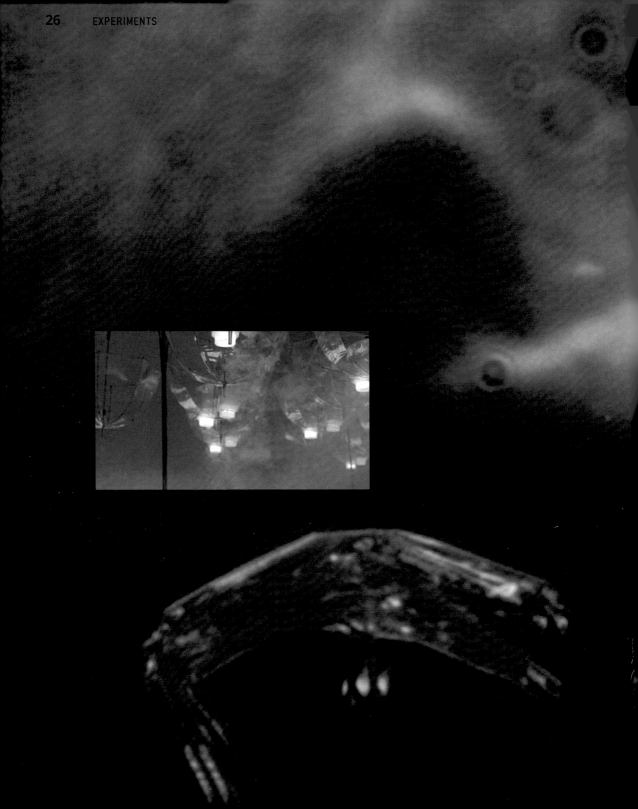

SET 2: Moving Air Systems

Test 2.1: Vents
[responsive environments]

Test 2.2: Fans
[robotic fabrication]

Test 2.3: Masks
[social prosthetics]

Leonardo da Vinci described in his *Notebook* the visual function of clouds when he suggested that "they are useful in filling up the gaps around figures, on the wall, to situate them in space just like angels and birds."[1] Today, public awareness of air spans environmental crises, health and safety measures, social and political acts, and so on. *Set 2* features investigations of designing with airflow as a material freely available in the environment. Titled *Test 2.1 FANS*, *Test 2.2 VENTS*, and *Test 2.3 MASKS*, this series of projects appear as fans looking like umbrellas, umbrellas that produce rain, and extra-large face masks (for two), respectively. Through interrogating cultural objects, these projects showcase a practice of translating fixed objects into synergistic systems with layers of familiarity that create poetic interactions between human and the altered homogenous medium. This set of experiments explores a cultural-environmental paradigm responding to phenomenological insights on visible forms of air and discussing its functions within and beyond specific spatial settings. The hurricanes, choreographic heat coils, and muted human breaths become inputs to the designed systems. By making the unseen medium perceptible, the works imagine the form, sequence, and rhythm of airflow as spatial agencies activating various sensorial and social events.

1   Marina Warner,
Phantasmagoria: Spirit Visions,
Metaphors, and Media into the
Twenty-first Century (Oxford: Oxford
University Press, 2006), 83.

[setups/linkages]

(Hot) Air on (and atop) Screens

The materials would be sounds, lights, gas, odors, etc. Things you can barely see, not ones you can grab. Through these elements you create new kind of spaces, which is not an architecture as we know it, but more of an environment, an atmosphere. They are materials of our times, what our society is producing.

—Doug Aitken and Francois Perrin

[layering]

Picture a fluffy cloud during sunset or a puff of steam in winter—ambiguous and ethereal forms in the air, varying in degrees of visibilities, have always dominated some of our most striking imaginations about the atmosphere. Da Vinci's notes on clouds refer to their function in static visual representations.[1] Artist and educator László Moholy-Nagy, on the other hand, once envisioned "unusual screens" made

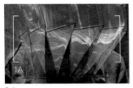

2.1

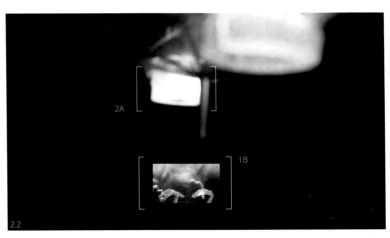

2.2

Fig 2.1. *Test 2.3 MASKS*, projection of forms of breaths on a translucent 3D screen in front of a person's mouth

Fig 2.2. *Test 2.1 VENTS*, kinetic air chamber (top), and *Test 2.2 FANS*, visualization of hot air produced by a robotic thermal device (bottom). Exhibition view, Wurster Gallery, University of California, Berkeley, 2020.

Fig 2.3. *Test 2.1 VENTS*, air puff exiting the umbrella outlet

Fig 2.4. *Test 2.1 VENTS*, air donut approaching the digital screen on the floor

of physical mediums such as fog, gas, and clouds for creating light visions in open spaces, turning the entire sky into a super screen as the ultimate media display that is—in media archaeologist Erkki Huhtamo's words—"tempting and evocative, but also unpredictable and elusive, resistant to closure and appropriation."[2] Used as integral visual figures in 2D illustrations of landscapes or functioning as media screens in the open air, drifting clouds or other visible forms of the medium present "a picture of the air as a force in play around its shape."[3] The imaginary yet scientific force-form play and its optical properties when intersected by light rays are some of the most powerful measures of movement and time, the appearance of which is a visual quantification of the otherwise imperceptible atmospheric dynamics.

Set 2 embraces the saturation of dynamic mediums and the visual synthesis of the atmosphere. Before being understood as scientific systems, this set of works is first visual apparatuses through which forms of airflow are not only produced but also perceived, signified, and interacted with. Visualizing airflow from the scale of an object to one of site-specific installations initiates various events of viewing, in which spaces are seen as layered devices of machines, air, and screens that afford the viewers opportunities to actively participate in the fluctuation of the environment—with human breaths proximally to hurricanes from afar.

So what are on the screens then? In this set of experiments, we observed three kinds of screen and airflow interplays. *Test 2.3 MASKS* is a wearable projection as well as a performance that translates biological signals into flow patterns as a language for social interaction. Projected from above onto a translucent 3D surface in front of the wearer's mouth, visualizations of human-breath fluctuations captured

and collide onto the rigid forms and surfaces of the device, which results in dynamic sculpted patterns—captured with a schlieren optics setup—only viewable on digital displays. Here, the screen reveals and frames visual narratives of wide plumes, vertical turbulence, and short spiral curves nodding, kissing, or punching one another. The robotic instruments, appearing to be strange characters dancing by themselves in front of a parabolic mirror, thus become part of an interactive current field.

Test 2.1 VENTS is a site-specific immersive exhibition that relates air movements at separate locations using responsive technologies. A suspended canopy of umbrellas produces "rain" of air puffs, which

Figs 2.1-2.4. Air/screen interplay and machine/air synthesis

[1A/1B > 3A/3B] forms of air on screens: mapped vs. framed vs. illuminated; [1B > 2A/2B] umbrellas vs. umbrellas: figural vs. actual

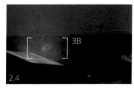

by wind sensors appear as fields of flowing currents that emerge, aggregate, intensify, and dissipate. As the physiological data changes while moving through spaces, the flow forms exaggerate the silent dialogue between human life and the built environment. The projection screen here serves as a mediator that reveals the muted impact the environment (as well as others) have on us, as evidenced through the air circulated by human lungs in terms of rhythm and intensity. *Test 2.2 FANS* is a series of robotic thermal devices that generates curvilinear and volumetric forms of air based on geometric logics. Streams of hot air emerge from heat coils that are set in motion around multiple axes and constantly rise, morph, bend,

are controlled by data input collected from the weather API (application programming interface), combining real-time local wind velocity and recorded speeds of Hurricane Florence in North and South Carolinas during September 2018. Designed for the group exhibition *SEE-ING*, *Test 2.1 VENTS* displays, below the umbrellas, digital monitors and large prints of works that distort a three-by-three grid.[4] As this grid creates irregular paths for viewing the exhibition, surprising alignments between digital media and the air outlet results. Light illuminating from the monitors portrays the volume of fog falling from above, which become air donuts that glow as they collide onto the screens. Or from another perspective, viewers look through the translucent, glowing veil to see the media looped on the monitor. The diffused imagery transforms the flat 2D digital screen into a haptic field, turning the choreography of air into a polyphony of light.

[synthesizing]

With titles referencing elements found in the HVAC industry, projects in *Set 2* narrate cultural perceptions of various instruments and objects by foregrounding the machine/air synthesis. Umbrellas, for instance, are one of the reoccurring figures—the function of the umbrella that sheds away currents (*Test 2.2 FANS*) and

units are constructed with ready-made products and customized connection joints, and the path of the fog as well as electrical systems are integrated into the assembly. Visual, audial, and tactile outputs from the mechanisms in operation as instructed by real-time data trigger various sensorial and interactive events. The encounters with fog rings—from seeing, to trying to touch, to moving around—lead to choreographed human movements based on the synergy of the visual media on display and the responsive atmosphere—a rediscovery of spectatorship in contemporary exhibition.

Like the making of air donuts, creating forms with discursive moving air that fills the void spaces

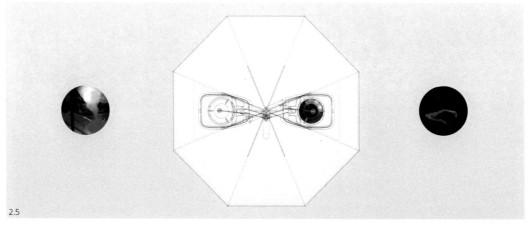

2.5

the dysfunction of the umbrella that produces rain (*Test 2.1 VENTS*).

From a scientific perspective, these machines are manifestations of the principles of physics. In *Test 2.1 VENTS*, each umbrella module of the array assembles a pair of kinetic air chambers onto its own structure. The chambers generate air-vortex rings that one can feel when they collapse onto the skin and a typological form of airflow widely used in both art installations, as well as the gaming industry, due to its visual and tactile properties. Pressure inputs injected through a plastic membrane into each air chamber result in the formation, movement, and morphing patterns of the air donuts. These umbrella

entails temporarily interrupting the entropic process to modulate its heterogeneity. With this logic, *Test 2.2 FANS* explores in-depth geometric attributes in flow articulations. A series of four devices is constructed following the principles of aerodynamic and thermal dynamics. Whether points of heat in space, or vectors of motion paths, or curvatures of rigid surfaces, these robotic instruments utilize heat and motion as agencies to print and sculpt while appearing to be automated props that actively participate in the crafted scenes on the digital screen. A smoking robot, a breathing cloth, or a pair of shaking umbrellas depict simultaneously the technological grounds and cultural imaginations of moving air systems.

Figs 2.7-2.8. *Test 2.1 VENTS 3.0*,
detail views of a drawing/machine
hybrid and of an interactive
installation with air/light/sound
effects

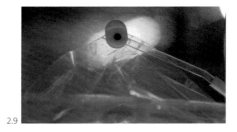

2.9

2.7

Fig 2.5. *Test 2.1 VENTS*,
umbrella-module drawing

Fig 2.6. *Test 2.1 VENTS*,
control-system diagram

2.6

2.8

Figs 2.9-2.10. *Test 2.1 VENTS*, detail
views of a plastic membrane attached
to a motor arm, and of human/fog ring
interactions

2.10

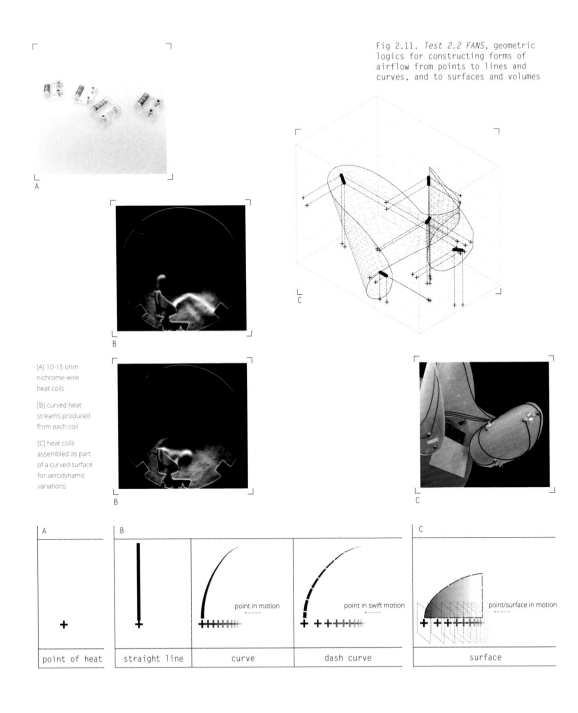

Fig 2.11. *Test 2.2 FANS*, geometric logics for constructing forms of airflow from points to lines and curves, and to surfaces and volumes

[A] 10-15 ohm nichrome-wire heat coils

[B] curved heat streams produced from each coil

[C] heat coils assembled as part of a curved surface for aerodynamic variations

A	B			C
+	**|**	point in motion	point in swift motion	point/surface in motion
point of heat	straight line	curve	dash curve	surface

[extending]

As visually manifested on the translucent screen, the breathing patterns in *Test 2.3 MASKS* show air as it flows through one's body and is expelled. The air surrounding us is an extension of the body. The inhale and exhale of it connect the internal organisms of separate individuals as a shared whole. With such invisible extensions, the measure of physical connectivity can thus be depicted by the mobility of the air, the range of its movements, and the proximity between breathing matters. This series of design explorations is not as much about air itself as it is about materializing the immaterial as part of the production of active systems, about building collective awareness through experimental architectural scenarios, and about signaling the shifting focus—from human-centric activities toward environmental sensitivities.

We need to rethink this connected field—the shared atmosphere. As we intervene within it, we disrupt, redirect, and participate as a part of it. We mediate material forms and this dynamic network—visually absent at large yet the most fundamental aspect of the physical world. In capturing and experiencing its flux, we overcome the limits of static vision and look at each present moment as a reflection of our own impacts.

[notes]

1   Cited in Marina Warner, *Phantasmagoria: Spirit Visions, Metaphors, and Media into the Twenty-first Century* (Oxford: Oxford University Press, 2006), 83.

2   Erkki Huhtamo "The Sky is (Not) the Limit: Envisioning the Ultimate Public Media Display," *Journal of Visual Culture* 8, no. 3 (May 11, 2010): 329–48. https://doi.org/10.1177/1470412910364291.

3   Warner, *Phantasmagoria*, 83.

4   *SEE-ING: the Environmental Consciousness Project* was a symposium and a group exhibition that took place at Lambla Gallery at University of North Carolina Charlotte between October 15 and November 16, 2018. See http://www.see-ing.net.

Figs 2.12-2.13. *Test 2.2 FANS*, four-bar linkage for printing and sculpting forms of airflow with high-frequency vibrations

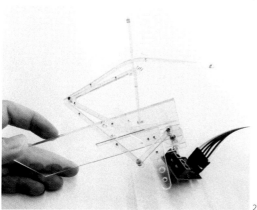

2.12

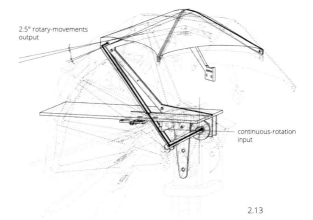

2.5° rotary-movements output

continuous-rotation input

2.13

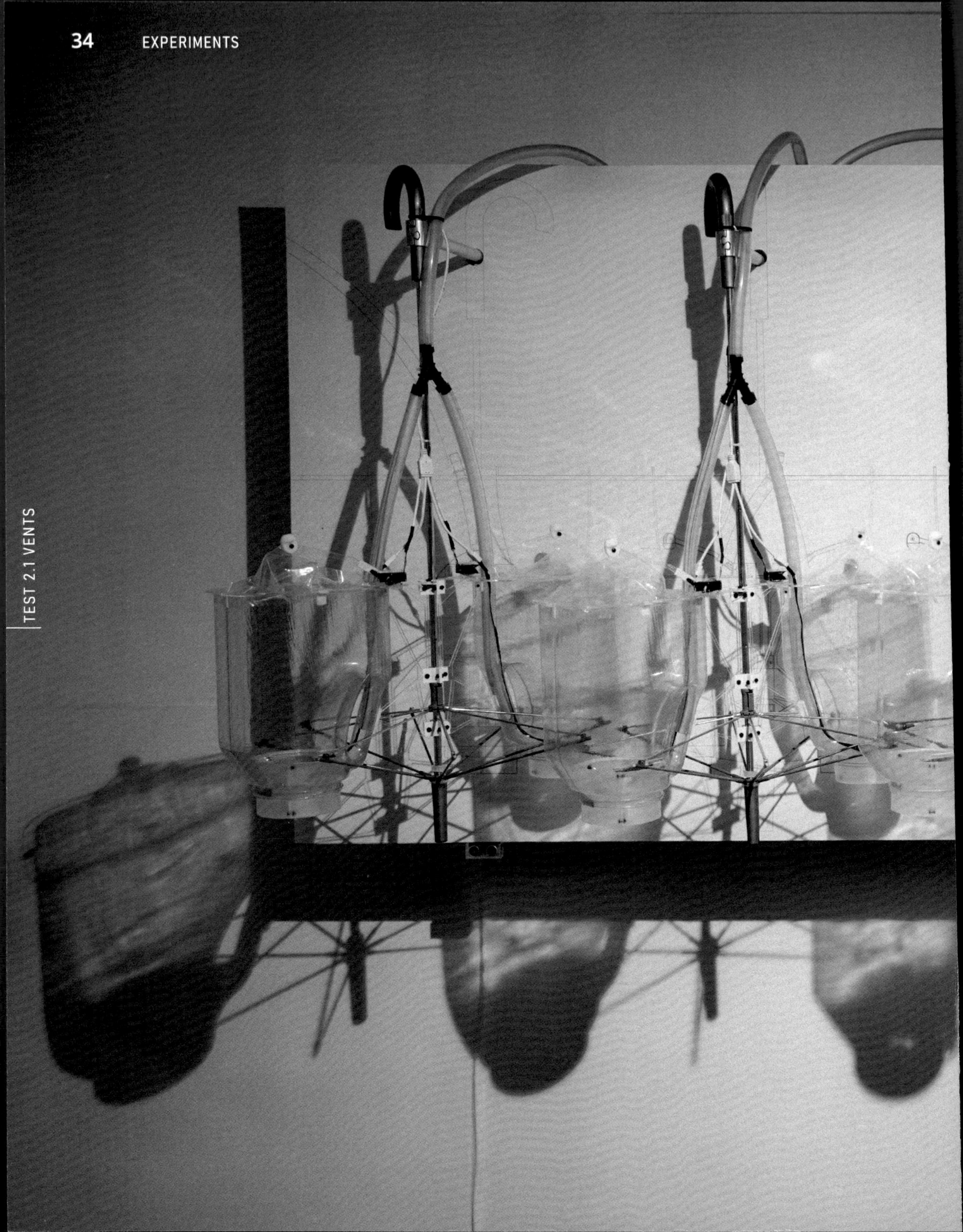

Fig 2.14. *Test 2.1 VENTS 3.0*, 'T' Space, Rhinebeck, NY, September 2022

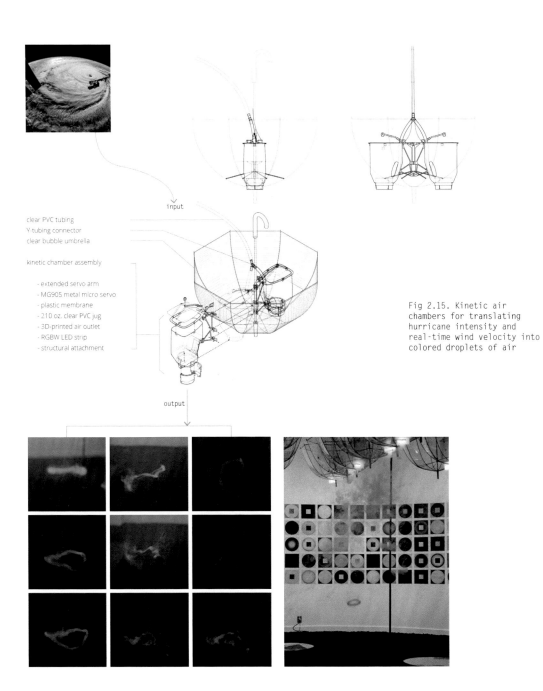

input

clear PVC tubing
Y-tubing connector
clear bubble umbrella

kinetic chamber assembly

- extended servo arm
- MG905 metal micro servo
- plastic membrane
- 210 oz. clear PVC jug
- 3D-printed air outlet
- RGBW LED strip
- structural attachment

Fig 2.15. Kinetic air
chambers for translating
hurricane intensity and
real-time wind velocity into
colored droplets of air

output

2.16

2.17

Figs 2.16-2.17. *Test 2.1 VENTS*, installation detail views, Lambla Gallery, University of North Carolina Charlotte, October-November 2018

[note 2.1]

Fog rings transform and enlarge as they fall downward to the floor. They become soft columns, constantly morphing due to the subtle forces caused by the movement and activities in the gallery.

[1] hang to existing structure
[2] 8'x8' existing lighting grid
[3] 1/2" PVC pipe painted black
[4] 4'x4' image frames
[5] 1" aluminum L channel
[6] 1" aluminum U channel
[7] 3/4" aluminum L channel
[8] to fog source

TEST 2.1 VENTS

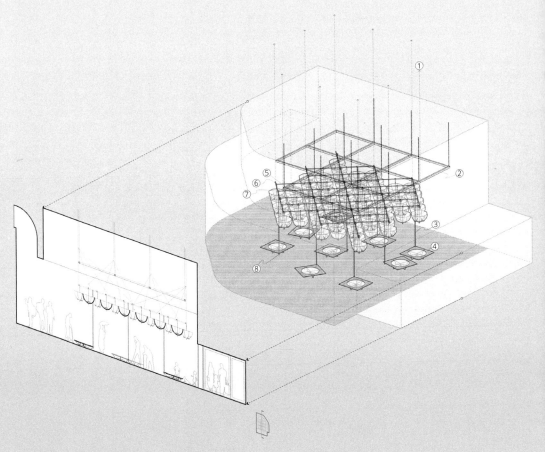

Fig 2.18. *Test 2.1 VENTS*,
installation design drawings

Fig 2.21. *Test 2.1 VENTS*,
installation view, Lambla
Gallery, University of North
Carolina Charlotte, 2018

Fig 2.19. *Test 2.1
VENTS 3.0*, installation
detail view, 'T' Space,
Rhinebeck, NY, September
2022

Fig 2.20. *Test 2.1
VENTS 3.0*, aftereffects:
volumetric light rays
visualized through human-
presence-triggered fog
outputs in the gallery

2.19   2.20

2.21

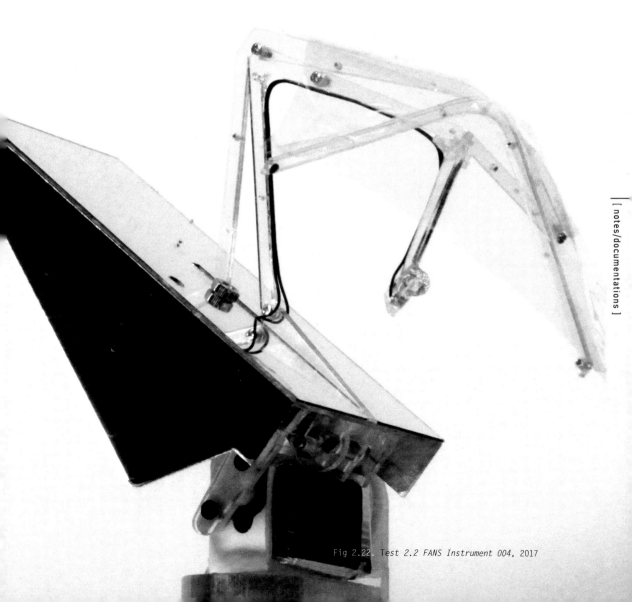

Fig 2.22. Test 2.2 FANS Instrument 004, 2017

2.23

Fig 2.23. Measured drawings of the
sculpted air, 2017

Fig 2.24. Test 2.2 *FANS Instrument
001* and *003*, exhibition view,
Wurster Gallery, University of
California, Berkeley, 2020

Fig 2.25. [opposite] Drawings
of four robotic thermal devices
that sculpt airflow

2.24

[note 2.2]

Measured drawings of the sculpted air, which
appears to be charcoal hand renderings, is in
fact a drawing experiment with computed pixels
defined by 2D coordinates on the digital screen.
The computational process translated optically
captured forms of airflow produced by *Test 2.2
FANS Instrument 003* into abstract patterns, and
the visual result was quantitatively produced and
embedded into the aesthetics of raster images.

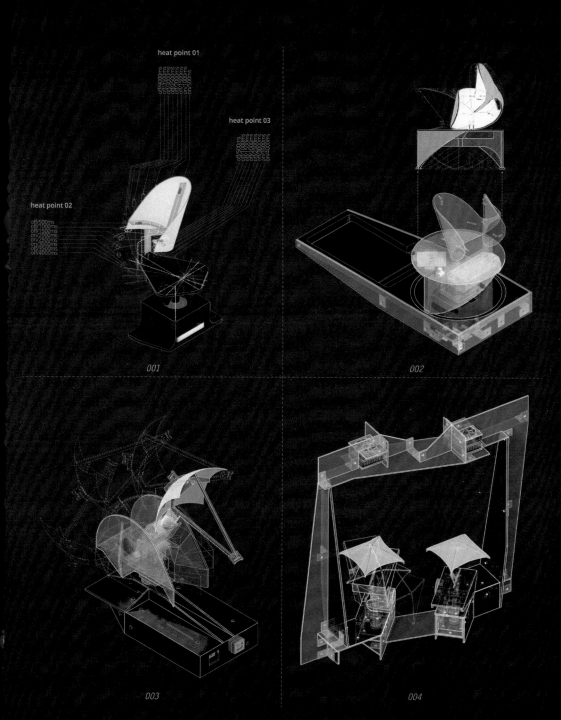

heat point 01

heat point 03

heat point 02

off/500ms
off/1000ms
off/1500ms
on/2000ms
on/2500ms
on/3000ms
off/3500ms
off/4000ms

001

002

003

004

Fig 2.26. *Test 2.2 FANS Instrument 004*, overview

Fig 2.27. [opposite] Printed and sculpted forms of heat

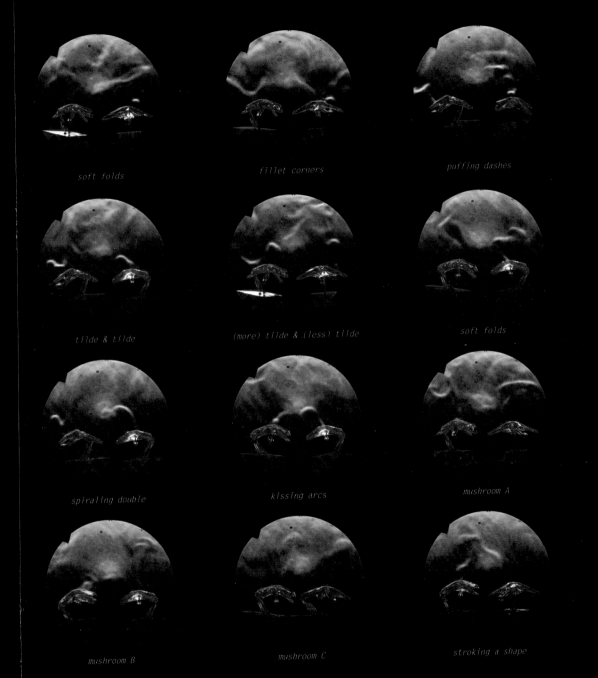

soft folds   fillet corners   puffing dashes

tilde & tilde   (more) tilde & (less) tilde   soft folds

spiraling double   kissing arcs   mushroom A

mushroom B   mushroom C   stroking a shape

[notes/documentations]

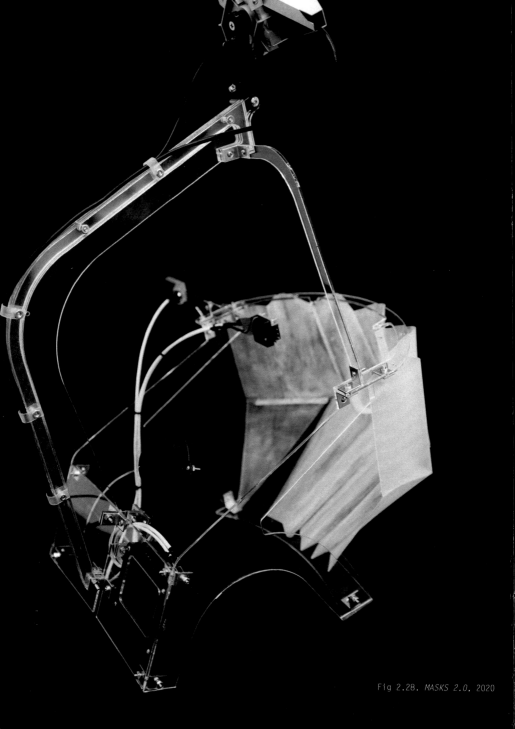

Fig 2.28. *MASKS 2.0.* 2020

[1] single-board computer
[2] microcontroller
[3] power bank
[4] cube projector
[5] breath sensor
[6] pulse sensor

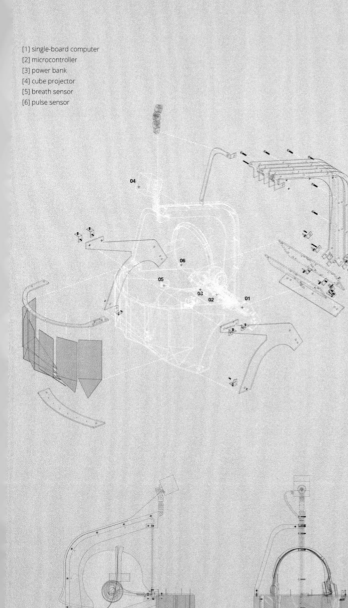

Fig 2.29. *Test 2.3 MASKS*,
drawings of initial prototype,
2015. (In 2020, it was
remodeled as a device for
two.)

[notes/documentations]

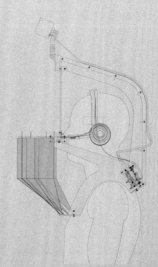

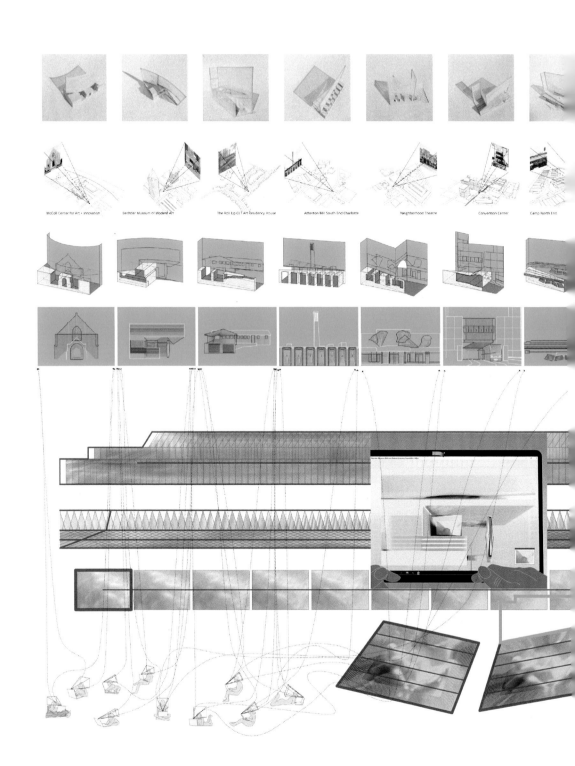

McColl Center for Art + Innovation   Bechtler Museum of Modern Art   The Roll Up CLT Art Residency House   Atherton Mill South End Charlotte   Neighborhood Theatre   Convention Center   Camp North End

SET 3: Video Captures and Screen Shares

Test 3.1:
Webcams+
[computational drawings]

Test 3.2:
Interior Cities
[interactive installation]

Test 3.3:
Collaborative-
vision Machines
[VR scanner bot]

In her article "Towards a Diffuse House," Anna Puigjaner states that the growing digital sphere has turned "the entirety of the built environment into an endless domestic landscape, one defined less by buildings or public spaces and more by objects and technologies."[1] In this vast digital sphere, physical bodies occupying one actual space at a time but simultaneously existing in—and being connected to—many others through cameras, networks, and screens has become the most iconic reality of the modern city. Since coronavirus shelter-in-place orders started taking place across the US in mid-March 2020, such a multiplicity of presence has spurred a cultural shift much more drastically than any that has come before. The pivot from the situated toward remoteness in social and professional lives urges new definitions of architectural boundaries, techno-aesthetics, domesticity, and public space. *Set 3* explores networked camera spaces as tools for placemaking, reflecting the short- and long-term shifts in living, working, and social-interaction modes since the beginning of the global pandemic lockdown. Designed with webcams, inhabitable screens, domestic archetypes, and daily-life activities, this series of experiments reimagines vision tools and computational mediums as architecture. They invite hybrid forms of engagement from the public, individuals, and nonhuman users when examining the world during and possibly after COVID-19 through interactive environments. These experiments question what existing architecture and digital media could offer in their radically transformed relationships with social mechanisms, humanity, and well-being.

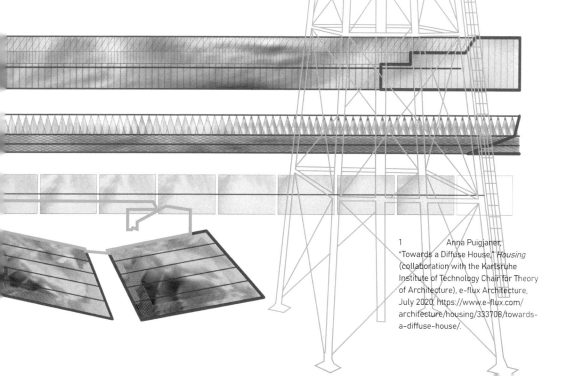

1   Anna Puigjaner, "Towards a Diffuse House," *Housing* (collaboration with the Karlsruhe Institute of Technology Chair for Theory of Architecture), e-flux Architecture, July 2020, https://www.e-flux.com/architecture/housing/333708/towards-a-diffuse-house/.

[setups/linkages]

Sticky Notes
over the
Camera

Screens themselves have the curious status of functioning simultaneously as immaterial thresholds onto another space and time and as solid, material entities....In so doing, they also put forth a rather unsettling proposition: that we are, quite literally, screen subjects—largely defined by our daily interactions mediated through a range of screen-based technological devices.

—Kate Mondloch, "Interface Matters"

[diffusing]

Today's rapidly popularized teleconferencing platforms might profoundly resonate with the traditional cubicle layout, which, since its beginning in 1964, has dominated workplace setups for decades. A visual correlation between the cubes of an individual's workspace and the flattened 2D boxes of camera views on digital

3.1

Fig 3.1. *Test 3.1
Webcams+*, rendered view
of folding mechanism
with a transformable
opening at the center
as a webcam cover

Figs 3.2-3.5. *Test
3.1 Webcams+*, webcam
drawing experiments
turning ordinary
objects and daily
life activities into
illusions of infinite
corridors, with
abstract color figures
appearing in motion

Fig 3.6. *Test 3.1
Webcams+*, rendered
webcam view of looking
through the opening as
the cover piece unfolds

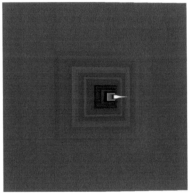

3.2

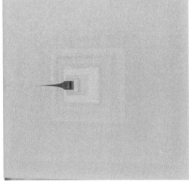

3.3

screens implies, in fact, quite obviously, a radical shift in modes of communication, from within shared spaces to via shared screens for exchanging data through machine-to-machine networks. In the era of remote communications and telepresence, personal spaces in professional lives have been increasingly seen as limited to areas in front of a webcam, presented through teleconferencing grids on digital monitors in many others' spaces at once. Consequently, personal spaces in the shared public domain—traditionally defined by walls or barriers within reachable proximities—are thus depicted as networks of framed camera views. Their static spatial outlines dissolve into fuzzy boundaries that dynamically recompose themselves at virtual distances in real time. Visual art and media scholar Giuliana Bruno argues in *Public Intimacy* that "in the modern era space could no longer be conceived as static and continuous" and that with cultural mobilization through new means of transportation and communication, our visual terrain has become disjointed, split, fragmented, multiplied, mobile, transient, and unstable.[1] The dominating visual territories of camera views, signifying characteristics of space as such, call for new design and representation logics for hybridized physical and virtual conditions that expand beyond physical limits. The disassociation of spatial connectivity from geographic locations signifies not only the dynamic and the fragmented, cinematic nature of the contemporary architectural experience but also the paradox of the increasingly nonrelated, contextless physical spaces and the necessity of their existence in the real world.

Set 3 consists of experiments that blur the distinction between inhabitable physical spaces and the perceptible virtual dimension through

concepts of the webcam and the screen sharing on teleconferencing platforms and develops a multimedia installation to instill hybrid forms of interactions. Using real-time webcam captures as inputs, the installation, which visitors could step into, constructs imaginary cityscapes interactively and transforms architectural objects and surfaces into inhabitable displays and interfaces. Test 3.3 Collaborate-vision Machines probes the intimacy between humans and technological devices by building a hybrid "eye" that perceives the built environment in motion. Virtual landscapes are created by perceptually stitching together the fragmented spatial information seen by the machine and modified by subjective human data.

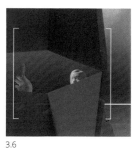

3.4

3.5

3.6

connecting, exchanging, and relocating within new image landscapes. Fluctuating the fusion of geometric and temporal parameters, such hybrid conditions capture, transmit, display, and interact with visual signals, through which ephemeral architectures emerge. Test 3.1 Webcams+ is a series of drawing instruments that use personal webcams to embrace the fuzzy edge as well as real time. Produced during the pandemic lockdown, the project imagines isolated personal spaces as screens and animations with algorithmic transformations of webcam captures, through which public spaces are reshaped as fictions of individuals—a play of overlapping the physical, the virtual, the personal, and the shared camera spaces. Test 3.2 Interior Cities borrows

Architect Toyo Ito once observed that space "no longer appears to be a vacuum in which solid bodies live, but rather a medium through which information is diffused."[2] Today, we live in a hybrid mode that foregrounds more visually than ever the diffused information of the personal level. Set 3 works extensively with such mediums to interrogate spatial boundaries and, by extension, the transformations of social relations at large that we are all taking part in.

[altering]

When it comes to the camera as an optical device that enables the recording of information through light, the capacity of hardware integration has drastically changed the notion of seeing. From photographer Eadweard Muybridge's multilens apparatus for scientific uses to depth sensors embedded in personal devices, the instrumented visual world has evolved and continues to transform before we can even notice. We can no longer perceive the built environment without being mediated through machine eyes. With advanced hardware and algorithms, vision systems intellectually mimic the coordination between human eyes and brains so as to measure, parse, store, translate, and display signals in visible forms. Design experiments in *Set 3* consider optical tools as critical agencies with both conceptual significance and

occurring around the webcam, such as peeling off the tape from the lens, adjusting lights, and moving hands between those objects while getting ready for video calls, reoccur frequently to fulfill work-from-home needs and beyond. These types of activities around the webcam serve as the main generators of visual inputs for customized drawing scripts and are reassembled computationally into surreal scenarios, appearing as dynamic, illusory textures overlaid onto existing built forms. Ultimately, the movements and objects over and around the lens transform the amount of visible area in the camera view; their dynamic proximity to the lens introduces a "room" that is only to be perceived through the camera, a temporary

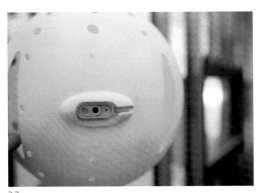

3.7

3.8

technical sophistication. These exercises curate active human engagements with captured visual information in examining and designing the new realities we reside in today.

Webcams for video streaming and network communications, for example—operating separate from advanced hardware—are often associated with low-res imagery, glitches, and low-bandwidth delays and most of the time bear concerns of compromised personal privacy. A front camera on a laptop nowadays is typically blocked by the user with masking tape of various colors or sticky notes, which has become a normal addition to the device. Both *Test 3.1 Webcams+* and *Test 3.2 Interior Cities* build on such cultural phenomena of the webcam. Routine actions

foreground that mediates between the flat screen and the viewers.

Therefore, exploring the webcam as a cultural object for interactive placemaking in these two experiments is to develop methods of playfully altering this "camera room" over time and numerically translating visual inputs into reordered 2D pixel arrays. Real-time video captures are stored temporarily, and still frames selected at certain intervals from the constantly updating sequences are outputted onto layered polygon shapes with remapped UV coordinates. Fictional forms emerged autonomously from the overlay of the current and successive series of stored prior frames. Just like the mechanical operation in photography with

Figs 3.7-3.8. *Test 3.2
Interior Cities*, two webcam
mechanisms designed as
suspended spheres

animated drawings from
real-time webcam inputs

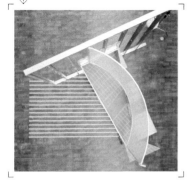

project onto
3D screens

Fig 3.9. *Test 3.2 Interior Cities*, color
schemes and line patterns calibrated for
producing hybrid material effects in motion
through webcam drawing script

controlled apertures over lenses—such as the slit-scan technique used in *Vertigo* (1958) or *2001: A Space Odyssey* (1968)—each series of sequential visuals collectively presents as superimposed and blurred frames, employing established pictorial techniques for "depicting the unfolding of time in visual terms."[3]

The interactive drawings produced with webcams are thus instruments of image and time. Whereas *Test 3.1 Webcams+* draws with the movements of masking tapes, sticky notes, hand gestures, and artificial lights around the webcam, *Test 3.2 Interior Cities* designs webcam mechanisms as huggable spheres, inviting visitors to get close, to look into them, to swing them around, to pet them, or to talk to each other around them, constantly generating changes in the captured views. Blocks of color appear as distorted doors and openings; objects partially blocking the lens create wall textures; hands waving close to the camera fluctuate the digital canvas with hues of reds. By mathematically indexing raster grids on which discrete pixels are captured and stored, webcam drawing instruments computationally alter the visual identities of reality.

[cocreating]

In enabling a person's active role in the process of compositing the physical and virtual worlds as a synthesized whole with technological objects as part, spaces become interpolations distributed between vision apparatus and screen interfaces. In constructing views to be captured by huggable webcams, the design of *Test 3.2 Interior Cities* plays with scaled-up grid-paper patterns and the form of folded sticky notes. With a sense of familiarity, these oversized objects produce material effects while offering seating functions. As one interacts with camera spheres, movement of the color and geometric patterns in captured scenes are then registered in the customized drawing scripts, translated into animated textures, and projected onto—and through—three-dimensionally configured screens. Thus, the installation is a 3D line drawing designed for the shared perception of humans and cameras, in which animations are coauthored by the human in motion and the camera's movements and

the viewing activities take place between the shared screen and the shared space.

Considering the function of dynamic visual information diffused within the built environment as such, spaces cocreated and cohabited by humans and machines are inhabitable images that embrace instability and process rather than symbolic forms. In *Test 3.3 Collaborative-vision Machines*, such images are produced by employing a multilayer framework to capture and computationally alter spatial data. A low-cost scanner bot is built to scan spaces along paths to produce "atmospheric" rather than "accurate" point clouds. A LiDAR sensor, a 360-degree camera, and a pair of VR trackers are parts of this mobile "eye," and through the collaboration, viewers virtually inhabit the captured visual environment with the scanner in motion. Real-time subjective data collected from sensors actively redraws the 3D scans, reconstructing the remote context as immersive point clouds. The integration of machine and human vision serves as a personal instrument that produces a perceptual diffusion, in which the scanner, human, and virtual imagery together blur the boundary of spaces defined by architectural surfaces and one's physical locations.

Hybridity and complexity of reality, in works as such, are experienced through the rhythm, speed, and sequence of the dynamic visual mediums, in which inhabitable forms emerge as part of the delay and glitch of webcams, or the fast-forward and slo-mo of the scanner bot. Video captures and screen shares are thus both technological acts for seeing together and are at the same time agencies for constructing synthetic realities that situate remoteness. And in experiencing the remoteness, we search for alternative forms of togetherness in architecture. As we imagine physical spaces to be inhabited via multipresence of the many, the design and representation need to consider an expanded vocabulary—namely, the seeable, the nonseeable, the filtered, the blurred, the communication activity, the background, the virtual presence within physical spaces, and so on—via teleconferencing platforms and beyond. From a simple piece of sticky note over the lens of a laptop camera to eye movements tracked through a headset, this set of works intends to collectively build toward an experimental visual system around such architectural qualities, through which we could rethink remote technologies and the architectures of the everyday.

[notes]

1   Giuliana Bruno, *Public Intimacy* (Cambridge, MA: MIT Press, 2007), 57.

2   Luigi Prestinenza Puglisi, *Hyper Architecture: Space in Electronic Age* (Basel: Birkhauser, 1999), 19.

3   Jimena Canales, "Desired Machines: Cinema and the World in Its Own Image," *Science in Context* 24, no. 3 (2011): 329–59. https://doi.org/10.1017/S0269889711000147.

3.10

Fig 3.10. Scanner bot, physical prototype

Fig 3.11. *Test 3.3 Collaborative-vision Machines*, a perceptual scan combining human inputs and machine measurements

3.11

Fig 3.12. *Test 3.1 Webcams+*. 2020

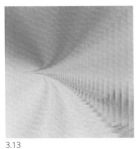

3.13

3.16

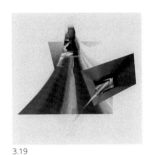

3.19

3.14

3.17

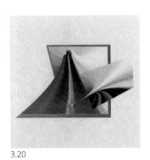

3.20

3.15

3.18

[note 3.1]

The visual, mechanical, and algorithmic transformations of cameras and images in producing these animations establish analytical relationships between camera apparatus and pixel arrays that translate chemical-mechanical methods of locomotion studies into raster-based operations. The interactive drawings turn a flat monitor into an interface that relates framed views of activities in front of the camera and the virtual "space" that appears to be inside the screen to the viewer's eyes.

3.21

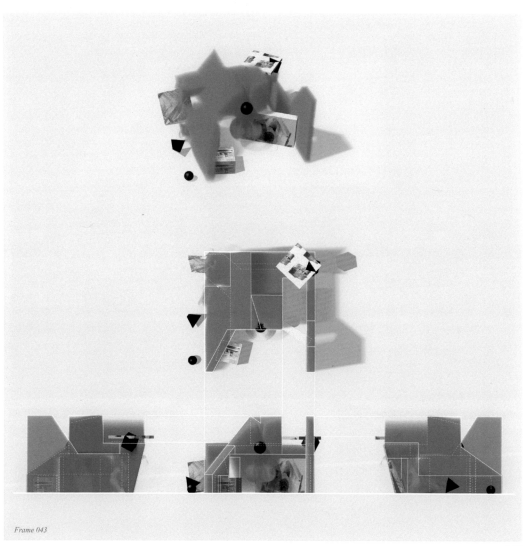

Frame 043

3.22

Figs 3.13-3.20. Webcam textures are interactively generated through drawing
scripts. Still frames excerpted from real-time interactive animation.

Figs 3.21-3.22. A fictional space of the new reality imagined with webcam
textures as animated texture maps, rethinking networked media, screen, and
virtuality in isolated physical spaces since March 2020. Still frames excerpted
from simulation video.

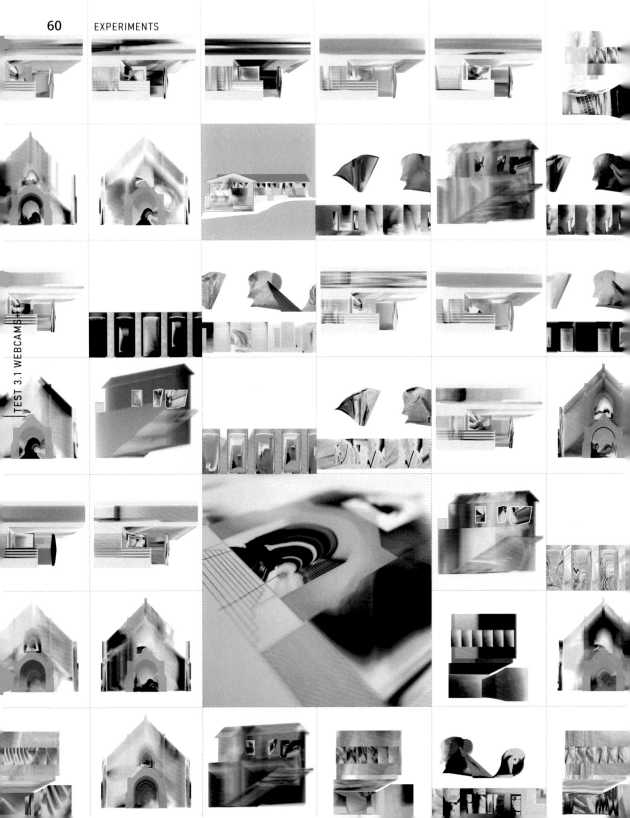

TEST 3.1 WEBCAMS

[notes/documentations]

Fig 3.23. Relating camera spaces: real-time video captures within personal spaces are mapped geometrically and temporally onto photographed built forms of the city.

TEST 3.2 INTERIOR CITIES

projection chamber #1
Blue Line/Charlotte Convention Center

projection chamber #2
Roll Up CLT studio

projection chamber #3
Camp North End

[note 3.2]

Test 3.2 Interior Cities applies webcam drawing techniques
to explore seven locations with diverse identities within
the city of Charlotte, North Carolina. These 3D-projection
chambers blur real and the virtual imagery to provide
a sense of familiarity and playfulness in a physical
environment that connects camera and screen spaces.
By transforming the camera views within the city into 3D
screens, real-time dynamic projections can be explored
from outside and from within.

Fig 3.24. *Test 3.2 Interior
Cities 0.0*, drawings and models
of seven inhabitable chamber
prototypes

projection chamber #4
McColl Center

projection chamber #5
Neighborhood Theatre

projection chamber #6
Atherton Mill

projection chamber #7
Bechtler Museum of Modern Art

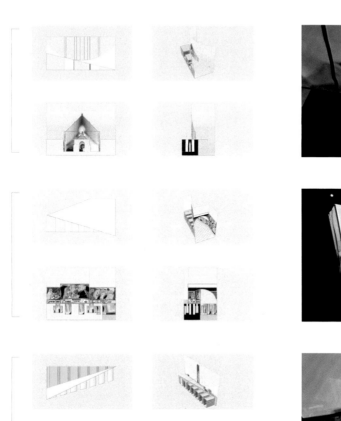

[notes/documentations]

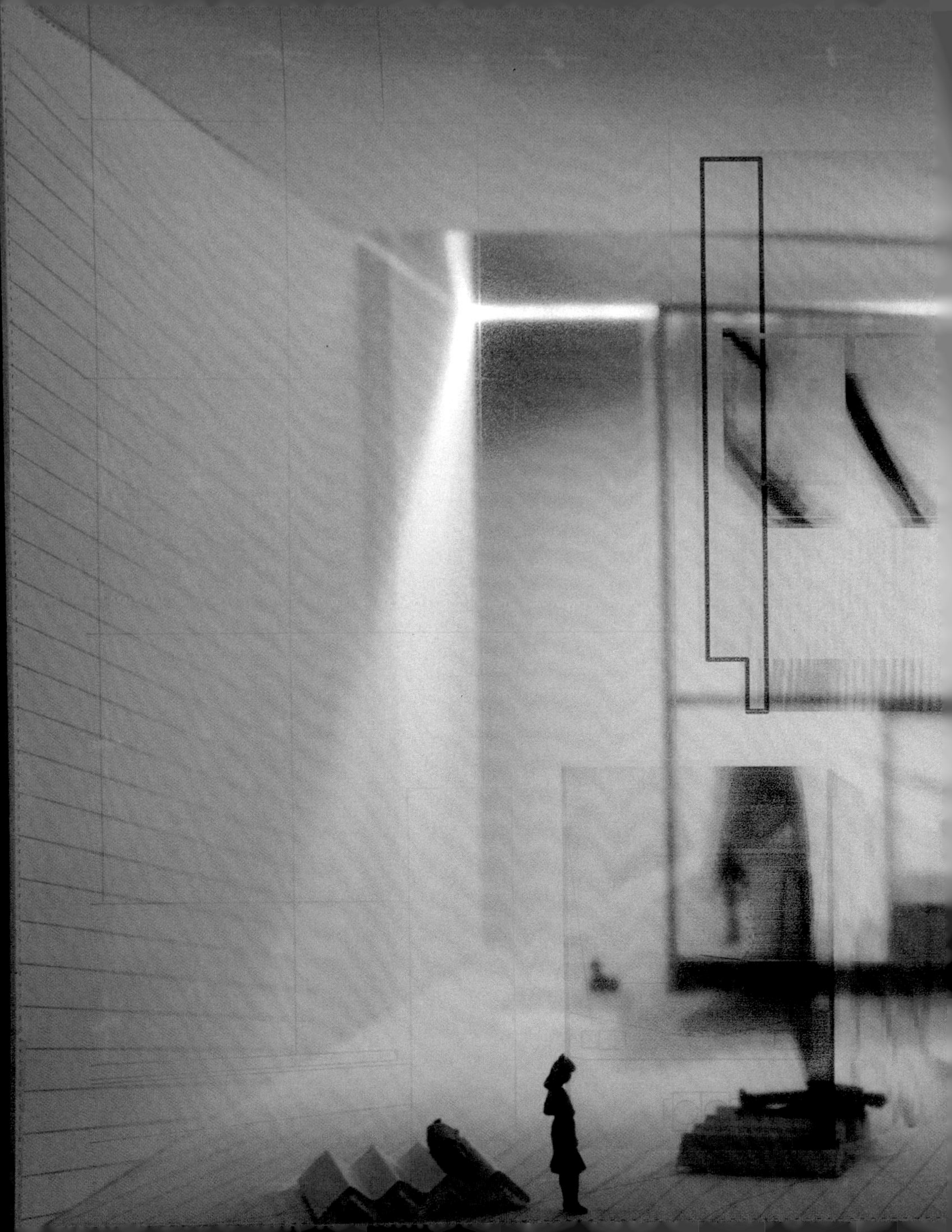

Fig 3.25. *Test 3.2 Interior Cities 0.5, 2022*

3.26

3.27

Figs 3.26–3.27. *Test 3.2 Interior Cities 0.5*, model/drawing hybrids as chambers with framed views, inhabiting the sight lines between one side and the other, and also as ontological abstractions of the digital screen, introducing ambiguity between the digital and the material, flatness and depth, as well as the act of "looking at" and the "looking through."

Fig 3.28. Suspended webcam
spheres act as interactive
spatial and computational
devices; scaled color sticky
notes and grid paper function as
furniture and as color inputs of
the real-time visual system.

capture   compute

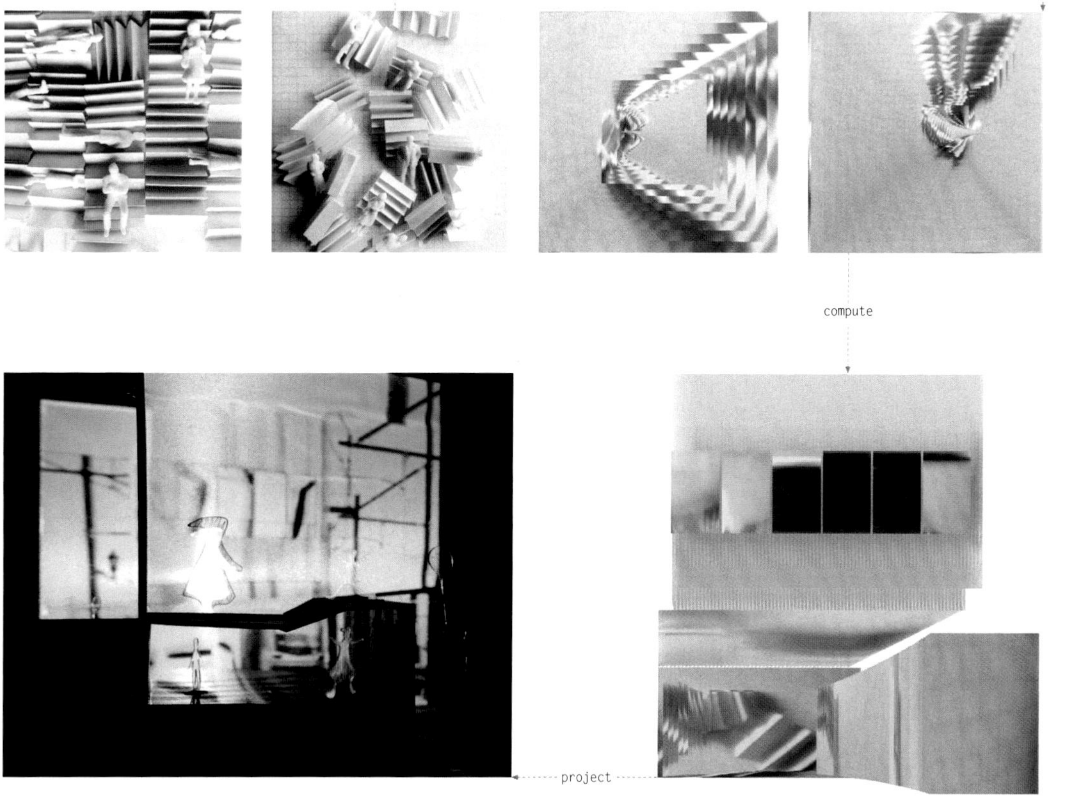

compute

project

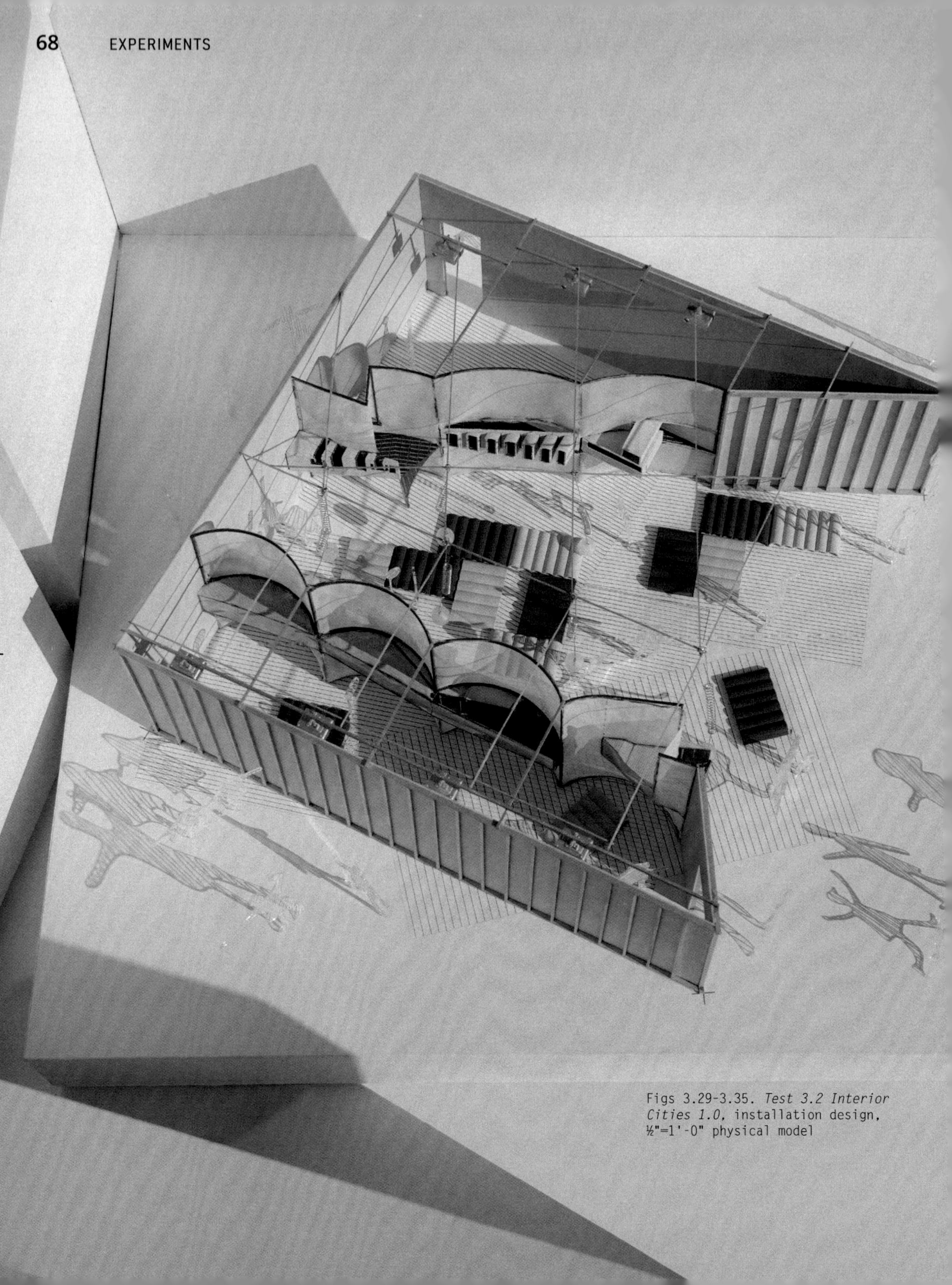

Figs 3.29-3.35. *Test 3.2 Interior Cities 1.0*, installation design, ½"=1'-0" physical model

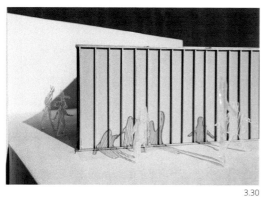

3.30

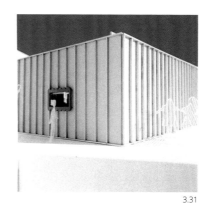

3.31

3.32

3.33

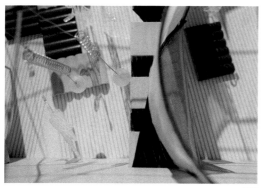

3.34

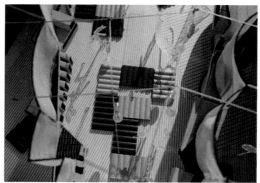

3.35

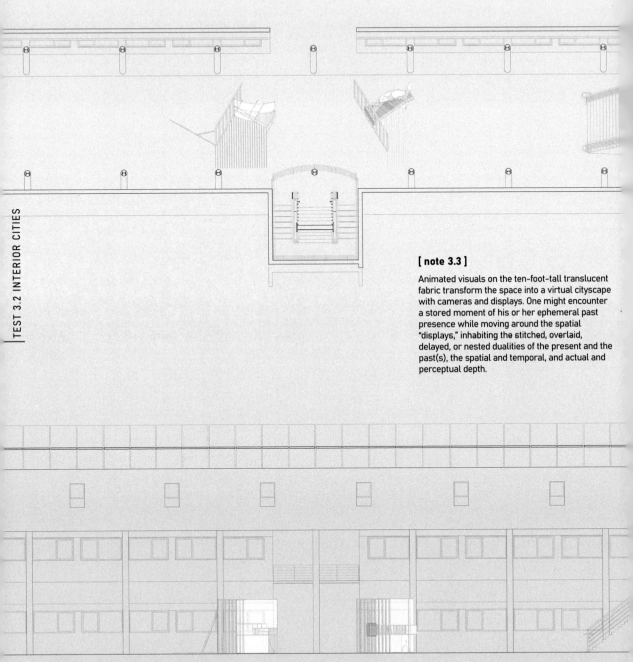

[note 3.3]

Animated visuals on the ten-foot-tall translucent fabric transform the space into a virtual cityscape with cameras and displays. One might encounter a stored moment of his or her ephemeral past presence while moving around the spatial "displays," inhabiting the stitched, overlaid, delayed, or nested dualities of the present and the past(s), the spatial and temporal, and actual and perceptual depth.

Fig 3.36. Full-scale-prototype drawings

3.37

3.38

3.39

3.40

Figs 3.37-3.40. *Test 3.2 Interior Cities 1.5,*
views of full-scale prototypes, Storrs Hall,
University of North Carolina Charlotte, 2023

TEST 3.3 COLLABORATIVE-VISION MACHINES

[note 3.4]

László Moholy-Nagy defined "vision in motion" as "a synonym for simultaneity and space-time; a means to comprehend the new dimension." Today, the perception of motion is collaborative and inseparable between human and machine. Here, through visual signals shared between the scanner bot and the viewer, traces and glitches recorded through the mobile machine eye became atmospheric animations as they receive human perception of motion as inputs.

Fig 3.41. Scanner bot 2.0

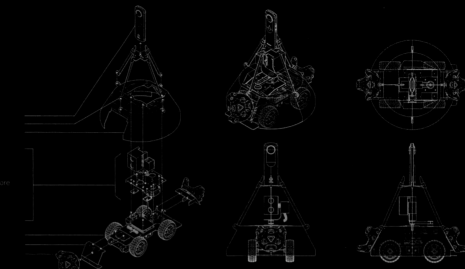

Ricoh Theta 360 camera
- 3D printed camera mount
- 3D printed shell

LiDAR mechanism assembly
- LiDAR Lite v3 scanner
- micro servo
- 3D printed 20-teeth 5mm bore
- timing belt
- Nema 17 stepper motor
- 6-wire slip ring

SunFounder PiCar-S
3D printed HTC Vive bracket
HTC Vive Pro trackers

Fig 3.42. *Test 3.3 Collaborative-vision Machines*, a perceptual scan, 2022

On Technological Models: Toward Something Big

In Conversation with Orit Halpern

[theorization/provocation]

Catty Dan Zhang: Starting from an overall picture of the built environment governed by computerized territories and supported by physical materials and infrastructure, we participate in and become part of the operations of all sorts of media spaces and computational systems, from phone apps to smart cities and automation. It is quite fascinating that in your work you engage various types and scales of technological models. And rather than assessing their effects, you trace their ontological infrastructures, and the theorization of these models becomes a model itself that leads to provocations and makes room for new forms of knowledge.

I would like to start off the conversation by capturing an overview of the motivation and methodologies that support such work. What is a technological model for you? How did you choose which of these models to study? What is their significance and relevance? What are some of the key relationships between their end effects and internal logics that allow them to provide a mode of integration and ideology?

Orit Halpern: To start, I usually tend to think that when we're thinking about digital technology, it is not about technology itself—for example, a phone as an object—but in terms of epistemologies. And epistemology is how we create worldviews. How do we make worlds—what is our perspective? What are the techniques and technologies that organize how we see? Most importantly, what are the structures and infrastructures that delimit what can be seen, said, done, or sensed? And I don't want to just keep it in the realm of the visual—but also, of course, what can be thought? There are obviously dominant models that constrain how we envision the future of technology.

And in the work I do, technology tends to be specific to whatever we're talking about. Whether it's a fiber-optic cable or a smart city, it is a particular infrastructure that has particular demands. In *The Smartness Mandate*

book, in thinking about the epistemology of smartness, I approached it like the story of science.[1] Like, how do we think about what kind of culture, what kind of practices, and what kind of materialities produce something that possesses *smartness*? When did intelligence or other figures of human agency or decision-making get transformed into this language—and into what effects? And in that sense, when I use the term *model*, I'm talking about being inside a world where we're deploying the term *smartness*—what are our ideas about, for example, in terms of an ecosystem?

So for me, when I say *model*, it's kind of a broader term, although it can include the model of a building or can actually deal with the experimental setup for which you determine parameters around a particular problem and then run a simulation. But in a broader sense, it's also about your general ideas about how a system works. So, for example, with environmental management discussed as a part of *The Smartness Mandate* book, I trace how people move from a cybernetic closed-world idea of the planet, from a report like *The Limits to Growth*—in which people envision a series of feedback loops that are depictable and a world that they can represent and manage if they just track all the flows of information from one entity to the next that could be somehow managed and perfectly calculated—to a model of a world that's kind of imbalanced.[2]

So nature's movement from predictability to imbalance sort of mimes and mirrors the geopolitical situation of the Cold War as networked and volatile, with the assumption that environments might constantly change, that they're actually not in this carefully managed and calculatable balance but rather are in constantly shifting phase changes, that there's the expectation of disruption as a regular event, and that systems won't return to what they looked like before, no matter what you do. For example, I have overfished cod on Georges Bank in Canada. When I stopped fishing, things didn't just jump back. They didn't go back. Something had happened. The system is complex, and something had changed in its balance and in the relationship between organisms, and the bank could no longer provide us with this service of codfish. Something else has to happen in order to get that ecosystem to operate as a fishing ground again.

That might seem like a really mundane situation, and maybe not that interesting, but fundamentally, what I mean when I say *model* is that models incorporate the parameters and assumptions we have about the world and set the bedrock of the kind of questions we're going to have to ask. So a question isn't, "How do we reach homeostasis in a resilient model of nature?" The question would be, "How do we manage the next disaster?" We're not going to stop the hurricanes, we assume they're coming, and we start building systems that adapt and learn in relationship to that event. Of course, that also means changing not only the techniques used in your model but also what you're building. Because now you can't assume that you can just put a sea wall there and it'll hold, that you only use concrete and do nothing else—you need to build an infrastructure that can somehow sense, respond to, and adapt to the changing water levels or whatever is happening because they're constantly going to change. Personally, I'm going to have to rethink really fundamental assumptions about how I've been managing the space, the territory, or the system to accommodate those changes. I guess that's what I mean by *model*, which is not so much a technology as it's an epistemology. It becomes a way of approaching problems, but, of course, that also includes how you build technologies.

[representation/attribute]

CDZ: In "Neural 'Freedoms': Population, Choice, and Machine Learning," you discussed the notion of the machine that was "engine not camera" and that intelligent models were "not supposed to show us what the process of learning looks like but rather be the process of learning."[3] And you wrote in the "Hopeful Resilience" article that the use of simulation or animation has now changed from prediction to speculation.[4] Although the contexts are very different, both arguments imply critiques of what is representable and what is to be represented in visual terms, and both suggest something about predictability. I was wondering if you could elaborate on the visual and representational challenges of technological models and which variables and attributes—whether visible or not—are important for a productive technical framework and consequently yield hopeful and responsible speculations of the future—either proposed by designers or dreamed by machine intelligence.

OH: Let's start with the question of representation. Of course, human beings need to represent stuff—that need just doesn't go away, although we dream about it. We want all sorts of neat things—unsupervised machine learning, data-driven decision-making—but ultimately,

which data you want to pick, how you ultimately set your parameters, even in large language-learning models, always comes back to having to put things in categories to give things ontologies, which leads to some form of representation. But for me, what's key here is not so much that this is a reality but that it's a really specific thing that people fantasize about not having to represent the world anymore—particularly sometime after World War II and really profoundly after the 1970s. And I think, for me, those moments mark critical time periods when we start understanding the performative nature of technologies, of our models, and of things like language or depiction. And we understand that models do not just represent something out there but also themselves do something that is actually world-making. Models are not merely laboratories that demonstrate something in the world—they actually make worlds.

Particularly with the rise of the internet, digital media, and AI, we live in a world that is reflexive and self-produced, right? Like there is Google Maps; there are all these GIS and GPS systems that represented the world outside. We're in these systems now, and they gather data about us, and that data starts to build the system that, for example, changes the way you are planning around traffic by transforming the kind of services available along that road or whatever. So we are seeing a kind of co-constitutive power coming into being. And in that sense, we're transforming our understanding of the work models do. So when Milton Friedman, who's a neoliberal economist, says that "a financial model is an engine, not a camera," what he is saying is that there are certain markets—like a derivatives market in which we're buying and selling debt or buying and selling currencies against each other into the future—that just wouldn't exist without computers and equations. It's not just out there matching supply and demand—it's actually a market about futures. It's that I'm buying and selling options on an asset before it's happened. That's a pretty remarkable shift in tense.

But in my book [*The Smartness Mandate*]—and I guess now I should really frame the centrality of political economy and finance to my thinking about *smartness* and of course to *models*—financial markets in many ways form the perfect place to see the most extreme tendencies of many of our technologies. For example, energy is one of the most heavily leveraged markets in the world. You know, at any moment there's like gazillion spot prices for oil in the world. And that's happening because people are betting on what the price of oil is going to be in two months, and three months, and six months. People are even building infrastructures according to future bets that will be bought and sold before we ever find out what actually happens. And for me, of course, that creates a lot of ethical questions: What does it mean to buy and sell the future before it happens? What kind of futures are you making? And are you basically leveraging or turning the future into debt in a way that doesn't benefit most of the world? And in carbon-based markets, that ambiguity of ethics becomes really visible.

You know, people are betting on wars right now. There are macro hedge funds betting on the Russian-Ukraine war. Rubles were super cheap [around March 2022], and people bought them up, expecting that they would go up. So they are actually banking in on the fact that there's geopolitical conflict. Do these forms of betting, in some sense, sell out the future by already making it bankable in the present? That's a kind of major question. But the issue is more that the financial markets also demonstrate something broader about smartness, platforms, and systems because all of those systems in certain ways are trying to derive more value out of an underlying asset. A famous one being Airbnb. Supposedly, there's all this unused real estate we're just going to put it to use, right? Airbnb doesn't build houses and doesn't manage properties; rather, it serves as a kind of platform and intermediary for matching this supposedly unused resource with a demand. The same thing happened with Uber, even though ultimately, we also understand that Uber created a certain condition for labor by getting all these people to work for them and cornering that labor market so that those workers could not ask for the same rights as if they were duly employed elsewhere.

So these kinds of models are, in many ways, extensions of this idea of derivation that comes out of finance, that they're deriving additional value. But moreover, they're always kind of doing it into the future. All of artificial intelligence is about managing futures, using past data to somehow extrapolate to find those patterns that'll tell us what people are going to do, how they're going to act, how we can bank in on it in the future and very often leveraging or selling the promise of that dataset. There are vast amounts of capital invested in the promise that somebody's got a great dataset to teach these machines to do things in the future or that's very valuable in terms of consumption or something else.

That's what I'm meaning here a bit about the transformation from prediction to speculation—because it's both about the fact that you're not really sure what's going to happen in the future, and you might not really care, which is an even more troublesome element. Or you do care, but not necessarily in ways that make a difference. Maybe you've heard terms like the "new normal" or other terms that indicate a lack of caring around the climate crisis. And there are all sorts of people, in geopolitical volatility, thinking, "Well, we had this model of globalization, now it's under the tank, and then there was a pandemic…" Increasingly, there's a sense that we can't really actually predict the future that well. So we have to develop strategies of resilience that can withstand these kinds of extremely volatile conditions, and it comes back to that environmental model I mentioned earlier. And that's kind of also the history of the derivative. In the seventies, it was the kind of supposed Keynesian Bretton Woods–based system and the kind of comfort, if you will, in a negative sense—I'm not saying that positively of the Cold War. Dissipated. With all this decolonization, different social changes, shifts to an information economy, people felt they just couldn't really predict the economy or the price that well. And they started creating technologies that literally allow you to hedge your bet, so that you could always put a dangerous bet with a safe one so that you could distribute your risks.

And I think that a dominant concept in platforms, artificial intelligence, and smartness in general is that people are clear that systems are really complicated and that they're not really sure what's going to happen, so they develop all sorts of ways to get value and not take on responsibility. It's like how Amazon didn't own any warehouses [until they shifted from leasing to purchasing]. And when Amazon ends up owning one too many vans, there's a New York Times article about now Amazon's vulnerable because labor unions can organize.[5] Now that they have distribution centers and drivers, and they're not using a third-party contractor—yeah, they've become vulnerable to traditional labor actions. But the logic of smartness is to try to avoid that, to create a decentralized and flexible system that allows you to evade chokepoints, stop bolts, or unpredictable events.

[algorithm/agency]

CDZ: You compared the heaviness of bearing the dense, infinite data accumulation with the lightness of being resilient and continuing to sustain. In "Hopeful Resilience," you discussed an analogy between cyberspace and the material environment by stressing the concreteness of the internet and the information that the transmission of data utilizing the sands and metals of our earth is not so different than constructing roads and buildings. And you also described that "derivation, extraction, and resilience are married in a manner that has turned the planet and all its forms of life into a massive medium for the development of smart technologies." In situating digital technologies in the environment, some of your recent work has been at the planetary scale, looking at the planet as a test bed and the landscape as a recording device, where "new forms of experience and cognition are no longer nested in single human bodies." If we recognize data as concrete, material as interface, planet as medium, mathematical model as infrastructure, etc., what is the necessity of individuals in relation to models and systems, and how is their agency leading to societal change in the material world? And what is our active role in working with large networks of humans and machines?

OH: These are amazing questions, and they're exactly what I need to find good answers to. There are a couple levels of responses. I guess I'll follow the scale idea. Let's take it at a big-level scale and then we'll dig down. *Planetarity* in general gets invoked by people like Dipesh Chakrabarty, who's a postcolonial historian, as sort of a term that might replace *globalization*, for one's understanding that globalization as we imagined back in the eighties or nineties was kind of a smooth space in which capital just flew around, goods just flew around, and everything just seamlessly got integrated into the interests of what we might call logistical capitalism of sorts. And planetarity actually understands that it's not quite like that; rather, there are many barriers and boundaries. There are tons of materialities from which toxic things have to get extracted by people. People are not allowed to move over every border and boundary. Nation-states are not over and might be taking some sort of new "extrastatecraft," to use Keller Easterling's manifestation.[6] There's actually a lot of disjuncture that logistical systems, supply chains, and things like that take advantage of—it's precisely that people don't get paid the same in every place that makes a lot of our manufacturing infrastructure organized the way it does, right? Like, actually activating or banking in on differences is bad, and in that sense, so are derivatives markets. I mean, you derive value from the differences between prices not from each thing, from the relationship between them.

There's something fundamental happening here. Planetarity is about synchronization; for me, it is about the synchronization of differences. So we can all experience the internet or the impact of artificial intelligences, or automation, or GIS/GPS—these are global phenomena virtually everywhere. But the impacts, the effects, and the relations are quite different depending on history, context, culture, and so forth. It's about a kind of nonhomogenized understanding that might still be able to count for something like, "Yeah, we're all on earth enduring the climate crisis, but obviously it doesn't impact everybody the same way." People of color in certain locations are impacted more negatively than those of us who have access to air-conditioned buildings. But planetarity is also about considering the geological and material, as well as the cultural, economic, and other things, together. I think that's why I think at a bigger scale; because right now, under the duress of contemporary geopolitics, the climate crisis, and shifting technologies, we need a framework that can bridge the material on social divides but also accounts for difference and homogeneity. That's how I put these things together. But at more specific levels, these systems are not monolithic. While I worry a whole lot about social justice and equity, I don't think that something like capitalism comes from above. In short, I think it's constituted by practices, techniques, technologies, institutions, organizations, and people. At the end of the day, whether the system is ChatGPT or a mine, there are people involved—it's not about machines. Machines are still programmed by somebody to do something, for someone, in the interest of certain organizations or groups.

In some sense, thinking about that gives us a new form of agency. If we think about systems in all their complexity and materialities, there are so many more places to act. And we participate in that acting through our work. We participate by building architectures for clients. We participate by building speculative architectures for no one but try to get people to imagine something differently. We are constantly negotiating these forces, obviously with different levels of power, but nonetheless, we are doing things. Above all, no matter how much data or how much stuff is flowing around the world, we always have to create value—which is to say, meaning—around different things. And what's most radically necessary is an understanding that there are always political battles over what is valuable: Why do we value automating one process over another? Why do we value the way we do real estate versus something else, like the maintenance of a coral reef, or what have you? These contests are constant, and we need to get involved in them not only by thinking about how values are produced but also about the fact that value is about meaning. And ultimately, it's also about narrative: How are we narrating and creating meaning around these models of systems? How are we narrating stories of agency? And that's a place where we do have a certain level of agency. And not only that, architecture plays a part in naturalizing, accepting, or making aesthetically pleasing particular relations of power, space, materials, money, and people—even though you don't usually think of a building or a structure as a narrative. There are a lot of opportunities to manipulate and think about, from how we visualize data, which is always a mode of storytelling and narration about the world, to how we think about how we interact and relate. For example, "material as interface" is really about how we construct our experiences with other beings in the world.

If we think about "the planet as a medium" as something that we're terraforming and geoengineering, as we are constantly, that might allow us to move away from questions of how to survive, which tends to justify a lot of bad activities, to questions of how we want to live, which is really different. What world do we want to build? What planet can we make possible? Do we want the one that we currently have, or do we need something else? And it comes down to the "mathematical model as infrastructure" as well. We are choosing the models, and we don't have to pick one we've selected in the past, we can change it. As long as computers aren't autonomously self-programming, all systems remain programmable and therefore changeable. I think that gives us a lot of agency, even if it's not the kind of imperialist colonial-like power from above to be like, "Here's my vision of the world, I will impose it." I think we need a kind of humble agency, one without ominations, in terms of thinking about the changes we can make.

[notes]

1   Orit Halpern and Robert Mitchell, *The Smartness Mandate* (Cambridge, MA: MIT Press, 2023).

2   Donella H. Meadows, Dennis L. Meadows, Jørgen Randers, and William W. Behrens III, *The Limit to Growth: A Report for the Club of Rome's Project on the Predicament of Mankind* (Washington DC: Potomac Associates, 1972).

3   Orit Halpern, "Neural 'Freedoms': Population, Choice, and Machine Learning" (lecture, ICI Berlin, March 27, 2023).

4   Orit Halpern "Hopeful Resilience," in *Accumulation: The Art, Architecture, and Media of Climate Change*, ed. Nick Axel, Daniel A. Barber, Nikolaus Hirsch, and Anton Vidokle (Minneapolis: University of Minnesota Press, 2022), 53–65.

5   Jodi Kantor, Karen Weise and Grace Ashford, "The Amazon That Customers Don't See," *New York Times*, June 15, 2021, https://www.nytimes.com/interactive/2021/06/15/us/amazon-workers.html.

6   See Keller Easterling, *Extrastatecraft: The Power of Infrastructure Space* (Brooklyn, NY: Verso, 2014).

Orit Halpern is the Lighthouse Professor and chair of Digital Cultures, as well as codirector of the Department of Speculative Transformation, at the Institute of Linguistics, Languages, and Cultural Studies, Technische Universität Dresden.

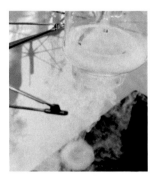

Fig 4.1. *Test 2.1 VENTS 3.0*, fog rings

Fig 4.2. [opposite] *Digital Air: Donuts*, still frame excerpted from simulation video

[acknowledgment]

Sincere thanks to Orit Halpern and Rebecca Uchill for their contributions. The following institutions supported the works in this pamphlet: the Graduate School of Design, Harvard University; the David R. Ravin School of Architecture, University of North Carolina Charlotte; the College of Environmental Design, University of California, Berkeley; 'T' Space and the Steven Myron Holl Foundation; and the School of Architecture, Florida Atlantic University. Deepest gratitude to Allen Sayegh, Krzysztof Wodiczko, Neil Gershenfeld, Giuliana Bruno, Andrew Witt, Panagiotis Michalatos, and Stefano Andreani for their advice and inspiration at the very beginning stages of this work. Thank you to my collaborators: Adam Pere on *Test 2.3 Masks*, Diego Camargo and Joseph Choma on the exhibition of *Test 3.2 Interior Cities 0.5*, Qi Xiong on *Test 3.3 Collaborative-vision Machines*, and Davis Owen on previous explorations with webcams. Thanks also to team members who lent their talents to various projects in this pamphlet: Pedro Piñera Rodriguez, Austin Johnson, Mahdi Ghavidel Sedehi, Rick Luu, Michael Allen, Menna Abdelghany, Anna Gelich, Torain Bullock, Cam Norris, and Arghavan Ebrahimi. The works in this volume came to fruition—intellectually and physically—with generous supports from and enlightening conversations with colleagues: Blaine Brownell, Rachel Dickey, Jefferson Ellinger, Thomas Forget, José Gámez, Lee Gray, Chris Jarrett, Ken Lambla, Marc Manack, Brook Muller, Dimitris Papanikolaou, Eric Sauda, Peter Wong, and the staff at the College of Arts+Architecture at the University of North Carolina Charlotte. Thank you to the jury of the Pamphlet Architecture 37 competition: Steven Holl, Kenneth Frampton, Kevin Lippert, Ioannis Oikonomou, Jennifer Olshin, Andrea Lee Simitch, and Eirini Tsachrelia.

This publication is dedicated to the memory of my grandparents, Zhang Sijing and Wu Meiling, my greatest life inspirations.

[image credits]

Fig 1.1, courtesy of Frank and Lillian Gilbreth Collection, Archives Center, National Museum of American History, Smithsonian Institution

Figs 2.3, 2.4, 2.9, 2.10, 2.17, photo credit Ben Premeaux

Fig 2.15 (bottom right), photo credit Milad Rogha

Figs 2.16, 2.21, photo credit Toby Shearer

Fig 3.9 (top views), photo credit Omar Awadallah

Copublished by the Steven Myron Holl Foundation and Station Hill Press. Steven Myron Holl Foundation, 60 Round Lake Road, Rhinebeck, NY, 12572, a not-for-profit, tax-exempt organization [501(c)(3)]. Station Hill Press is the publishing project of the Institute for Publishing Arts, Inc., 120 Station Hill Road, Barrytown, NY, 12507, a not-for-profit, tax-exempt organization [501(c)(3)].

Support for *Pamphlet Architecture 37* is generously provided by Elise Jaffe + Jeffrey Brown.

Cover images: *Digital Air: Donuts*, 2020

Copyediting: Linda Lee
Design: Temporary Office

Library of Congress Cataloging-in-Publication Data available upon request from the publisher

[pamphlet architecture]

Pamphlet Architecture was initiated in 1977 as an independent vehicle to criticize, question, and exchange views. Each issue is assembled by an individual author, architect, or collective. For information, Pamphlet proposals, or contributions, please write to info@smhfoundation.org or go to www.pamphlet-architecture.com.

Pamphlets published:

[1] *Bridges*
S. Holl, 1977*

[2] *10 California Houses*
M. Mack, 1978*

[3] *Villa Prima Facie*
L. Lerup, 1978*

[4] *Stairwells*
L. Dimitriu, 1979*

[5] *Alphabetical City*
S. Holl, 1980

[6] *Einstein Tomb*
L. Woods, 1980*

[7] *Bridge of Houses*
S. Holl, 1981*

[8] *Planetary Architecture*
Z. Hadid, 1981*

[9] *Rural and Urban House Types*
S. Holl, 1981*

[10] *Metafisica della Architettura*
A. Sartoris, 1984*

[11] *Hybrid Buildings*
J. Fenton, 1985

[12] *Building: Machines*
R. McCarter, 1987

[13] *Edge of a City*
S. Holl, 1991

[14] *Mosquitoes*
K. Kaplan, T. Krueger, 1993

[15] *War and Architecture*
L. Woods, 1993

[16] *Architecture as a Translation of Music*
E. Martin, 1994**

[17] *Small Buildings*
M. Caldwell, 1996

[19] *Reading Drawing Building*
M. Silver, 1996**

[20] *Seven Partly Underground Rooms*
M. A. Ray, 1997

[21] *Situation Normal...*
Lewis.Tsurumaki.Lewis, 1998

[22] *Other Plans*
Michael Sorkin Studio, 2001

[23] *Move*
J. S. Dickson, 2002

[24] *Some Among Them Are Killers*
D. Ross, 2003

[25] *Gravity*
J. Cathcart et al., 2003

[26] *13 Projects for the Sheridan Expressway*
J. Solomon, 2004

[27] *Tooling*
Aranda/Lasch, 2006

[28] *Augmented Landscapes*
Smout Allen, 2007

[29] *Ambiguous Spaces*
Naja & deOstos, 2008

[30] *Coupling*
InfraNet Lab / Lateral Office, 2010

[31] *New Haiti Villages*
S. Holl, 2011

[32] *Resilience*
Stasus, 2012

[33] *Islands and Atolls*
L. Callejas / LCLA Office, 2013

[34] *Fathoming the Unfathomable*
N. Chard & P. Kulper, 2013

[35] *Going Live*
P. Bélanger / OPSYS, 2015

[36] *Buoyant Clarity*
C. Meyer, S. Meyer, D. Hemmendinger, 2018

*out of print, available only in the collection *Pamphlet Architecture 1–10*
**out of print, available only in the collection *Pamphlet Architecture 11–20*